A History of Ulster County Under the Dominion of the Dutch

BY

AUGUSTUS H. VAN BUREN

KINGSTON, N. Y.

1923

J. C. & A. L. Fawcett, Inc.
Publishers

38-01 23rd AVENUE
ASTORIA, N. Y. 11105

TO my wife: It is long, long ago since you placed your hand in mine and gave yourself to me. Many years have flown. During them all you have had but one thought, the welfare of myself and of the children who came to us. Without your love, your devotion, your self-sacrifice, your assistance, your never-failing faith in me, this work never could have been accomplished. So, I dedicate, I consecrate, this book to you. May the good Father keep and protect you. May he strew the path you shall trod with every blessing and be with you to the very end.

CONTENTS

ULSTER COUNTY UNDER THE DUTCH
CHAPTER I.
THE RED MEN

THE English named the Indians, who occupied the greater part of New Jersey and Delaware, and the valley of the Delaware river in Pennsylvania, after that river upon whose banks, near the site of Philadelphia, blazed their council fire.

They proudly called themselves Lenni-Lenape (original or pre-eminent men). Their Totem was the wolf from which the French called them Loups (wolves).

The Indians, inhabiting Ulster County and the adjacent regions, belonged to the Munsee (at the place where stones are gathered together) tribe, one of the principal divisions of the Delawares. They occupied the head waters of the Delaware and the west bank of the Hudson from the Catskills to the borders of New Jersey. Their principal band was the Minisinks (the place of the Minsi), who occupied the southwest part of Ulster and Orange counties and the adjoining parts of New Jersey and Pennsylvania.

The other bands were the Catskills, Mamekotings, Warwarsinks, Waoranecs, and Warranawonkongs.

They were called the five tribes of the Esopus country.

These were the "Esopus Indians," whose war-whoops terrified the Dutchmen at Esopus; who laid Wildwyck in ashes and who battled for their hunting grounds against the troops of Martin Cregier. The Catskills had their principal village just north of the Esopus creek. In all probability they were the Indians mentioned in the journal of Henry Hudson:—"At night we came to other mountaines, which lie from the river's side. There wee found very loving people, and very old men; where wee were well used."

The Warwarsinks were located in the town of Warwarsing, at or near the junction of the Warwarsing and the Rondout creek. The name probably means:—"At a place where the stream bends, winds, twists, or eddies around a point or promontory." Other authorities give the meaning:—"Many hollow stones," referring to stones hollowed out by the action of the creek. The Mamekotings occupied Mamakating valley west of the Shawangunk mountains. The word probably means:— "the place at or on a very bad hill."

The Waoranecs were located at the mouth of Wappingers creek and around the cove or bay at the head of Newburgh bay. The Warranawonkongs was the principal band of the Esopus Indians. They had a village in the town of Shawangunk and another in the town of Warwarsing. Their wigwams stood at and about Wildwyck, now Kingston. They frequented the mouth of the Rondout creek.

The names of the two last above bands are probably derived from a word signifying:—"hollowing, concave site." "Cove." "Bay." Descriptive of Newburgh bay and the mouth of the Rondout creek.

Each of these bands had its main village where their forts were erected. These were defended by three rows of palisades and the houses in the fort encircled by thick cleft palisades with port holes in them, and covered with the bark of trees. During the summer and fall they roamed over the surrounding country in search of game and built their temporary huts wherever trade, the chase or fancy called them.

Two main trails led from the Delaware to the Hudson river. One began on the Neversink creek near Port Jervis, ran through the Mamakating valley and struck the Rondout creek near Napanoch. Then down that stream to Marbletown. Then across to the Esopus creek and down the same to its mouth at Saugerties. The other crossed the mountains at Minnisink to the valley of the Wallkill and followed that and the Rondout creek to the Hudson at Kingston.

Many paths led from the one trail to the other, traces of these remain to this day. Long before the advent of the white-man the Indian warriors silently trod these trails in search of their enemy and beside these paths they lay in ambuscade awaiting their foe. It was at the end of these trails, at the mouth of the Esopus and the Rondout, that they stood gazing in fear and in wonder at the ship of Hudson beating its way up the river that was to bear his name.

In the valleys through which ran these trails they pitched their wigwams, planted and cultivated their crops and pursued the deer and the bear in the surrounding forest.

Down these trails came the Indian Braves armed with gun and with hatchet to lay in ruins the settlement of the white-man at Esopus, and over them they fled back to their mountain fastness.

The mode of life, the habits and customs of the Indians are too well-known to require description here. Only those disclosed by the records as characteristic of the Esopus tribes are here alluded to.

The tribes were divided into clans or families, each having its chief. The names of some of these families have been preserved, as the Amogarickakan family, the Kettsypowy family, the Mahon family, and the Katatawis family.

They did not subsist upon the chase alone. They cultivated their fields. They raised large quantities of corn and vegetables, which they stored in the ground for winter use. Monianac (Indian corn of Maize) was their main food supply.

Martin Cregier, who destroyed their villages after the burning of Wildwyck in 1663, states that his troops cut down, near one of their forts, about two hundred and fifteen acres of growing maize and burnt above a hundred pits full of corn and beans. Here is a description of their management of the corn crop and the uses to which they put it, written in 1628.

"At the end of March they begin to break up the earth with mattocks, which they buy from us for the skins of beavers or otters, or for sewan. They make heaps like molehills, each about two and a half feet from the others, which they sow or plant in April with maize, in each heap five or six grains; in the middle of May, when the maize is the height of a finger or more, they plant in each heap three or four Turkish beans, which then grow up with and against the maize, which serves for props, for the maize grows on stalks similar to the sugar cane. It is a grain to which much labor must be given, with weeding and earthing-up, or it does not thrive; and to this the women must attend very closely. Those stalks which are low and bear no ears, they pluck up in August, and suck out the sap, which is as sweet as if it were sugar-cane. When they wish to make use of the grain for bread or porridge, which they call Sappaen, they first boil it and then beat it flat upon a stone; then they put it into a wooden mortar, which they know how to hollow out by fire; and then they have a stone pestle, which they know how to make themselves, with which they pound it small, and sift it through a small basket, which they understand how to weave of the rushes before mentioned. The finest meal they mix with luke-warm water, and knead it into dough, then they make round, flat little cakes of it, of the thickness of an inch or a little more, which they bury in hot ashes, and so bake into bread; and when these are baked they have some fresh water by them in which they wash them while hot, one after another, and it is good bread, but heavy. The coarest meal they boil into a porridge, as is before mentioned, and it is good eating when there is butter over it, but a food which is very soon digested. The grain being dried, they put it into baskets woven of rushes or wild hemp, and bury it into the earth, where they let it lie, and go with their husbands and children in October to hunt deer, leaving at home with their maize the old people who cannot follow; in December they return home, and the flesh which they have not been able to eat while fresh, they smoke on the way, and bring it back with them. They come home as fat as moles."

The Dutch called the Indians who were not chiefs "Barebacks," alluding to the fact that during the summer season they wore no clothing on the upper part of the body. To return the compliment the Indians called the Dutch "Schwonnacks," signifying "people of the salt water," because the Dutch had come over the sea.

They had their festivals, social gatherings, dances and general jollifications, called "cantico" or "kintacoy." The use of this word, descriptive of a dance, any social gathering or a drunken carouse, lingers among the descendants of the Dutch in Ulster County to this day.

The Indians had a "Tennis-Court" near the corner of Hone and Pierpont streets in the city of Kingston. It is mentioned by Thomas Chambers in a letter written in 1658.

One of the favorite games of all the Eastern tribes was played with a small ball of deerskin stuffed with hair or moss, or a round piece of wood, with one or two netted rackets somewhat like tennis rackets. Two goals were set up at a distance of several hundred yards from each other, and the object of each party was to drive the ball under the goal of the opposing party by means of the racket, without touching it with the hand. Two families or two tribes played against each other. The game was attended with dancing and feasting, and the stakes ran high. This undoubtedly was the game played at the Tennis-Court mentioned by Chambers. The Indians used this game as a stratagem to obtain entrance to Ft. Mackinaw in 1764, of which Parkman gives a vivid description in his "Conspiracy of Pontiac." It was adopted by the Canadians as their national game, under the name of la crosse.

Great misapprehension exists as to the status of the Indian woman. She is usually pictured as a mere beast of burden, a hewer of wood and a drawer of water for her husband and the family. It is true, she did the household work, tilled the fields and gathered the crops, but to no greater extent than do the peasant women of Germany, France, Holland and Russia. It is no infrequent sight, even at this day, to see women laboring in the fields in the land of the Esopus.

Some of the clans had a chieftainess who ruled and governed them. Her word was law. One of these, Nipapoa, held sway over a band of the Catskills. On her wigwam was painted the figure of a wolf, the totemic emblem of her tribe. She was part owner of Campels Island, lying south of Albany. In 1661 she joined in a deed of the same to Andries Herbertsen and Rutger Jacobsen. In 1677 the chieftainesses Wawawamis and Mamaroch join in a deed to Louis DuBois and his associates of land at New Paltz.

The women had a voice in the council of the tribe. Even in the weighty matters of war or peace they were consulted.

In 1660 the Esopus chief, Seweckenamo, while engaged in negotiating a treaty of peace with the council at New Amsterdam, stated that he had spoken with the women about it. Had asked them what they thought best and they had answered that they desired peace; "that we may peacefully plant the land and live in peace."

Women's rights and the rights of women were well recognized. It was not necessary for the squaws to organize a suffragette party. They usually got what they wanted. The secret of their great influence probably lay in the fact that each of them was an excellent cook and each wife became the mother of a lusty brood of papooses.

The names of a number of the chiefs appear of record. Occasionally a fact or incident concerning them lights up these old Dutch annals.

Preumaecker. He, with other chiefs, ceded lands at Wildwyck to Governor Stuyvesant in 1658. He was the oldest Esopus Sachem.

Seweckenamo. He was one of the chiefs in 1658 at

the time of the cession of lands at Esopus to Stuyvesant. He signed the treaties of peace of 1660 and 1664. In 1665, with other chiefs, he executed a deed conveying lands at Esopus to Governor Nicolls. As evidence of the execution of the deed the chiefs delivered to the governor two small sticks and in the name of their "subjects," one of the "subjects" delivered to Nicolls, "two other small, round sticks in token of their assent." In return Nicolls delivered to the chiefs "three Laced Redd Coates." He was one of the Esopus Sachems who conveyed lands at New Paltz, sixteen miles south of Wildwyck, to Lewis DuBois and his associates in 1677.

He was instrumental in having the prisoners taken at Wildwyck in 1663 returned to their homes. After the war of 1664 he appeared before the council at New Amsterdam, pathetically told the sorrows of his people, and asked that provisions be sent to them as they had nothing to live on.

Kaelcop. (Baldhead.) In 1659 he warned "Kit" Davis to move away from the strand as the Indians intended to attack the whites. He was a party to the above treaty of 1660. In 1677 he, for himself and the Amogarickakan family, and Ankerop for himself and the Kettsypowy family, executed a deed of the remaining lands of the Indians at Esopus to Governor Andros.

Ankerop. He evidently was cautious in executing deeds or binding himself by treaties, for his name seldom appears appended to such instruments. He owned lands in the town of Warwarsing as late as 1699. In 1680 he was living in the town of Rosendale, about eight miles south of Kingston. In that year Jacob Rutgersen leased land in that town to Dirck Keyser. The lease provides:—"The lessee shall, during the lease, permit Ankerop to plant four schepels of maize, and shall plow for him two days in the year, but as soon as Ankerop is dead Dirck Keyser shall be exempt from the same."

In 1677 Governor Andros granted a patent to Lewis DuBois and his partners of a tract of land at New Paltz which they had purchased of the Indians in the same year. Some doubt arose as to the exact location of one of the corners of the patent. So in 1722 the justices of the county asked Ankerop to point it out. The old Indian took the magistrates "to the high mountain, which is named 'Maggrnapogh,' now the famous summer resort, 'Lake Mohunk,'" and pointed out the corner.

What a spectacle. There on the mountain summit stood the old chief. Beneath him, on the one side, the valley of the Wallkill. On the other, the valley of the Rondout and the Esopus. There had stood the villages of his people. There, waving, tossing in the summer breezes, their fields of maize. There, the women had tilled the fields and the children laughed and played amid the daises and the flowers. Over the trails, crossing these very mountains, he had led his braves to the chase and to war. Gone. All gone now. The white man had taken them all. What must have been his thoughts as the sun went down, and hill and valley, forest and stream, slowly faded into the shadows.

After the destruction of their villages in 1663 the Indians lived in peace with the whites. At the outbreak of the Revolutionary War but few were left in Ulster County.

Most of them had left the valley of the Hudson and were living in the Indian village of Oquaga, near the site of Binghamton. In 1778 the Iroquois, the allies of the British, made this village their headquarters. In the same year the Americans, under Colonel Butler, attacked and destroyed the village. Their homes gone, a portion of the Esopus clans joined the Oneidas and moved with them to their reservation in Wisconsin. Most of them journeyed down the Susquehanna and joined the Delawares. The march of the white man forced the Delawares into Ohio, Indiana, Missouri and finally, in 1867, to the Indian territory, where they were incorporated with the Cherokees.

Few memorials of them remain in Ulster County.

Occasionally, the plow turning over the sod upon which once stood their wigwams, brings to the surface their stone arrow heads and hatchets. In the town of Esopus, on the shore of the Hudson, the figure of an Indian chief is cut in the rock. Two plumes adorn the head. One hand holds a wand, the other a gun. So he stands, forever gazing over the waters upon which his people paddled their canoes.

Here and there, a locality, stream and mountain, still bear the names the red men gave them.

Esopus is from Sepu, "river" and —es "small."

Honk Falls, a falls on the Rondout creek in the town of Warwarsing, is from Hannek, "a rapid stream."

Kerhonkson, a village in the town of Warwarsing, is probably derived from "Gahan," "shallow, low water."

Koxing Kill, a stream in the town of Rosendale, from Koghksohsing, "near a high place."

Lackawack, a settlement in the town of Warwarsing, from a word meaning "The Fork," "Fork of a river."

Meenahga, the name of a hotel on the Shawangunk mountains, a forced rendering of Mih'n-acki, "Huckelberry land."

Napanoch, a village, from a word meaning "Water land, or land overflowed with water."

Shandaken, a town, from "Schindak," "Hemlock Woods," Schindaking— "At the hemlock woods," or place of hemlocks.

Shokan, a village in the town of Olive, now covered by the waters of the great reservoir the City of New York has constructed from a word meaning, "Outlet or mouth of a stream." Ashokan is a pronunciation.

Warwarsing, from a word meaning "At a place where the stream winds, bends, twists, or eddies around a point."

Mohunk, the famous summer resort on the Shawangunk mountains, is probably from Magonck or Magunk, "a great tree." The word appears in various forms: Moggoneck, Magg onck, Moggonock, Maggrnapogh. A great tree may have stood on or at the foot of the mountain where Ankerop stood when he pointed out the boundaries of the new Paltz patent.

Shawangunk, now the name of a town, a stream, and the mountain range extending through the southern part of the county, was originally applied to an indefinite tract of land situated in the present towns of Gardiner and Shawankunk, lying between the Shawangunk Kill and the mountains. It is probably from Shawan, "South." South mountain. South water. South place, or from Shaw, "Side" —ong, "hill" and —unk "At" (or on) the hill side.

For many years an old Indian lived in a shanty on the bank of the Rondout creek, a mile or so above the city of Kingston. He died there in 1830. He was buried beside his hut. He was the last of the Esopus.

A monument has been erected to the memory of Thomas Chambers, the first white settler in the land of the Esopus.

Why should not a shaft be reared to the memory of the Indians? To perpetuate the names of Preumaecker; Seweckenamo; Ankerop; and that old baldhead, Kaelcop. They were pure Americans. They were the first settlers. They owned the land. They battled for their homes, though they were but wigwams. They fought for their wives, though they were but squaws. With dauntless courage, they faced death for their children, though they were but papooses. All honor to them. To every one of them.

CHAPTER II.

THE COMING OF THE WHITE MAN

THE first settlement within the limits of the present county of Ulster was made at Esopus. Where and whence Esopus?

In 1614 some merchants of Holland, who had sent ships to trade in the lands discovered by Henry Hudson caused a "Figurative Map" of the same to be made. They laid it before the State's General and requested and obtained a special charter giving them the exclusive right to visit and navigate to the same. On this map, on the east side of the Hudson, at about the latitude of Catskill, is the name of a tribe of Indians, the "Waronecks," and just below is the word "Esopus."

In 1624, Nicolaes van Wassenaer, writing of the Indians inhabiting New Netherland, says: "Near one place, Esopus, are two or three tribes." In 1688, Catelyn Trice, an old French woman, made her deposition in which she states that she came to this country in the year 1623, in the ship Unity, and, "When as ye ship came as farr as Sopus, which is ½ way to Albanie; they lightened ye ship wth some boats y^t were left there by ye Dutch that had been there the year before a trade-ing wth ye Indians upont there oune accompts & gone back again to Holland & so brought ye vessel up."

In 1625, Johannes de Laet, of Leydon, a director of the West India Company, published his "New World or Description of West India." In describing the Hudson he says:—"This reach (covering Newburgh Bay) ex-tends to another narrow pass, where on the west side of the river, there is a sharp point of land that juts out, with some shoals, and opposite a bend in the river, on which another nation of savages, the Waoranecks, have their abode, at a place called Esopus. A little beyond, on the west side, where there is a creek, and the river becomes more shallow, the Waranawankongs reside; here are several small islands."

The ship Rensselaerswyck left Amsterdam September 25, 1636, arrived at Manhattan March 4, 1637, and sailed up the river as far as Fort Orange. The log book of the ship, under date of March 31, 1637, records:—"In the morning the wind was about s. w. with fair weather. We got under sail and came to the esoepes. In the eve-ning the wind changed to the north and blew hard." Under date of June 4, 1637, on the voyage down the river, the record is:—"It was calm and we drifted along with the ebb tide and came before the groote esopes. There we got a steady breeze and sailed down the lange rack." David Pieterszoon de Vries sailed up the river to Fort Orange in 1640. In his account of the voyage he says:— "The 27th (April) we came to Esoopes, where a creek runs in; and there the savages had much maize land, but all somewhat stony." He left Fort Orange May 14th and says:—"And the same day reached Esopers, where a creek runs in, and where there is some maize land upon which some savages live."

Van Der Doncks map of 1656, of New Netherland, shows the "Groote" Esopus river and also the "Cleyne Esopus."

Esopus is from the Indian Sepu, "River" and —es, "small." As first used it was applied to an indefinite territory on the east side of the Hudson. About 1623 it was localized at the mouth of the Rondout creek; from which it was extended and applied to several streams; to the Dutch settlement Wildwyck, now Kingston; and to all the surrounding country and to the Indians inhabiting the same.

The date of the first white settlement at Esopus has been a much mooted question. As the matter is of considerable interest the evidence relating to it is here given.

At Fort Orange, on the 5th day of May, 1652, two Indians, "living in the Esopus," conveyed to Thomas Chambers a "parcel of land situated in the Esopus."

The Indian trails from the head waters of the Delaware River to the Hudson terminated the one, at the mouth of the Esopus Creek at Saugerties, the other at the mouth of the Rondout at Kingston. These two localities were frequented by the Indians. There can be but little doubt that the Dutch from Fort Orange and New Amsterdam, at a very early period, visited the same for trade with them. It is not at all probable that Chambers and those who came to Esopus with him would purchase land in and remove to a place of which they knew nothing. Chambers must have visited the lands he purchased before the execution of the deed. He was a practical, level-headed Englishman. He would not buy a pig in a poke. There is no evidence of any settlement, or of an attempt to found one, within the present territorial limits of Ulster County, prior to this deed to Chambers.

Neither the Figurative Map of 1614 or Van Der Donck's of 1656 show any settlement. Neither Wassenaer, de Vries, de Laet, or the French woman Trico, mention a settlement or use language from which it can be inferred that there was one. This is also true of the log book of the ship Rensselaerswyck. From 1646 to 1654 Chambers occupied a farm in Rensselaerswyck Manor which he leased from van Rensselaer, the Patroon. His account with the Patroon runs from 1646 to 1666. It contains the following entry:—"This day, 14 July, 1654, Thomas Chambers has delivered to me his farm with house, hay barracks and barn and have I released him from his contract. Thomas Chambers in the Esopus."

There are but very few entries in the account after the above. On November 18, 1654, the patroon leases the same land to Jan Barentsz Wemp, showing that in July, 1654, Chambers had given up the farm and was at Esopus.

A deed from Abraham de Lametter to Wilhelmus Hoghtiling conveying twelve acres "at or near the Rondout upon the strand of the Esopus Creek," states that Johannis Dykmand bought it from the Indians and conveyed it to Christopher Davis, August 16, 1653. Confirming this on June 11, 1663, the wife of Davis in a petition to Stuyvesant states that Johannes Dykman had granted the land to Davis in 1653; that his dwelling had been burned by the savages; that he had been compelled to abandon the property and asks that he be allowed to again take possession and that he have a deed for it.

The order of Governor Stuyvesant made May, 1661, erecting the settlement at "the Esopus" into a village states that it had been inhabited six or seven years.

The Fort Orange minutes of 1654, state that a letter had been sent to the Director-General about the excise and the lack of grain measures here, at Katskil and in the Esopus.

On September 30, 1654, a resolution was passed to send a yacht to the Manhattan and another to the Esopus for help against the Indians said to be hostile.

In 1654 a patent for about sixty-five acres at Esopus was granted to Juriaen Westphael. On February 2, 1661, Jan Verbeck and Francis Pietersen testified at the request of Evert Pels that they were both present in the spring of 1654 when Pels and the late Jacob Jansen Stoll divided the land bought by them of the Indians at the Esopus.

March 27, 1657, Johanna de Hulter, in her petition for a patent for lands at Esopus, states that her deceased husband had applied for a patent for the same November 5, 1654.

September 25, 1656, a patent for seventy-two acres of land "opposite to the land of Thomas Chambers" was granted to Christoffel Davids.

During September, 1655, the Indians made an attack on New Amsterdam. This caused great alarm throughout all the colony, and the settlers in the outlying towns fled to New Amsterdam.

That there were settlers at Esopus at this time and that they joined in the general exodus is evidenced by a letter from Jacob Jansen Stoll to Stuyvesant, dated April 12, 1658, in which, apologizing for the small quantity of grain he sends the Governor, he says he has done the best he could and:—"besides I have got a little behindhand through the last flight." Also by a letter from Thomas Chambers to Stuyvesant dated "Great Aesopus,"

May 2, 1658, asking that troops be sent for protection against the Indians:—" as we have been driven away once before and expelled from our property and it begins anew now." Also by the fact that in May, 1658, at the time of the building of the stockade at Wildwyck, the settlers told Stuyvesant that they would be ruined men, "if they were now again, as two or three years ago, obliged to leave their property." Also by an order of the Court at Fort Orange in 1656 for contributions for a present to the Indians for ransoming prisoners taken at the Esopus.

From all the above it may be safely asserted that the first settlement in Ulster County was made at Esopus in 1652 or 1653.

Many of these pioneers came from the Manor of Rensselaerswyck. That princely domain, embracing most of the present counties of Rensselaer, Columbia and Albany except Fort Orange and the land lying immediately about it; over which the Patroon, Kilian van Rensselaer, ruled a feudal lord.

Why did they come? Mayhap it was the wanderlust that lay in the blood. Perhaps the fertile valley of the Esopus Creek, ready for the plow, attracted them. Perchance there was a broader, a deeper reason. The patroon was the chief magistrate of his estate. From the decrees of his courts there was practically no appeal. He had the first right to purchase the products raised by his tenants who must grind their grist at his mill and could not hunt or fish without his license. The tenants of the manor farms were, in large measure, but the vassals of the patroon. Perhaps it was to escape all this, to own themselves, that they left Rensselaerswyck.

Perhaps it was their desire to be able to put their foot down upon a spot of ground and say to all the world, this is mine, that induced them to come to the land of the Esopus.

CHAPTER III

THE PLANTING OF ESOPUS

EXCEPT the fact that its inhabitants had abandoned their homes at the time of the attack by the Indians on New Amsterdam in 1655, we have no record of the settlement until 1658.

They had then built their houses and barns and cultivated the fields. They were ready to battle with the wilderness, with its wild beasts and with the Indians. In this year their troubles with the red men began. On the first of May, 1658, a group of Indians had gathered at their tennis court or ball field near the Rondout Creek. They had a ten gallon keg of brandy. It was pure brandy, for Thomas Chambers tasted it, and Chambers knew good brandy. Perhaps they had a ball match and were celebrating. At all events, they got very drunk and about dusk:—"they fired at and killed Harmen Jacobsen, who was standing on the yacht of Willem Moer." During the night they set fire to the house of Jacob Adrijansen. He, with his wife and children, and Andries van der Sluys, who lived in the family, fled to the yacht of Moer. The body of poor Jacobsen was taken on the yacht of Louwrens Louwrensen to Manhattan and there buried. As a sequel to this sad story, Stuyvesant and his council, at the request of the bereaved widow, Marretje Pieters, certified under the seal of the colony that Jacobsen was:—"accidently shot by a drunken Indian or savage who stood on the shore opposite the yacht." The widow evidently desired to rid herself of all that would remind her of her husband, for on May 7, 1658, the court at New Amsterdam appointed Hendrick Janzen vander Vin and Abraham Staats to take charge of the estate of Jacobsen because his widow had "laid the key on the coffin" and "the estate left by him has been kicked away by his wife with the foot," thus testifying that she would have nothing to do with it and had turned it over to his creditors.

The Indians grew more insolent and aggressive. They

held fire brands under the roofs of the houses declaring they would burn them if the whites did not plow their land which they were compelled to do. They taunted them with their weakness and contemptuously declared if they killed one of them they could pay for it in wampum. They called them dogs and threatened to burn their houses. They did not dare leave their dwellings. The fields lay idle. The news of all this, with appeals for help, had been sent to Stuyvesant.

On May 18, 1658, Jacob Jansen Stoll, Thomas Chambers and others sent Stuyvesant a joint letter calling his attention to the importance of the settlement, telling him of the conduct of the Indians, their defenceless condition and imploring him to at once send troops for their protection. On May 28 the council at New Amsterdam directed Stuyvesant to at once proceed to the Esopus with fifty or sixty soldiers. The governor and the troops set sail the next day.

They reached the mouth of the Rondout Creek the next day. It was low water and the yacht of Stuyvesant ran aground. A messenger was sent to several Indians whose huts stood on the bank of the creek, asking them to come aboard the yacht and another to tell the settlers of the arrival of the governor.

Very shortly Chambers and Andries van der Sluys, who had been anxiously looking for the arrival of the governor, came on the yacht accompanied by two of the Indians. Stuyvesant assured them that he meant none of them any harm. He had come to ascertain the cause of the trouble between the Indians and the whites. Induced by some presents, they promised to go notify their chiefs to meet the governor the next day at the house of Jacob Jansen Stoll to talk matters over. Then Chambers told the governor of all the depredations of the Indians, mournfully concluding that since they had written him the savages had killed "two sows, being with pig" belonging to Stoll. By this time the yachts bearing the soldiers had arrived. They quietly disembarked, and headed by Chambers, all marched to his house, where they remained over night. We may be sure that the keen eyes of the Indians were watching them as silently, without the beat of drum, they climbed the hill. The same hill down whose slope, over two centuries later, marched the boys in blue of Ulster County on their way to the battlefields of the South.

The next day, May 30, the troops marched to the home of Stoll, it being nearer the huts of the Indians. It being Ascension Day, divine service was held. In the afternoon Stuyvesant met the settlers. He talked straight to the point. The harvest season was coming on. It was no time to make matters worse by attacking the Indians. He could not protect them as long as they lived separately, their dwellings scattered here and there contrary to the orders of the company. It was absolutely necessary that they at once move together where he could assist them with a few soldiers. They must either do this or move to Manhattan or Fort Orange, or, they would do neither, they must defend themselves. They conceded that a concentrated settlement was necessary, but everyone proposed his own place as being most conveniently located. They urged that the buildings could not be moved before harvest time. They earnestly requested that the soldiers might remain until the crops were gathered. To this Stuyvesant would not agree. He told them they must make up their minds. That he and the troops would remain until the place for settlement was inclosed with palisades, provided they went to work at once. They asked time for consideration, which was granted. The next day, May 31, 1658, the inhabitants signed the following agreement:—

"We, the undersigned, all inhabitants of the Aesopus, having from time to time experienced very distressing calamities and felt and discovered, to our loss, the unreliable and unbearable audacity of the savage barbarous natives, how unsafe it is to trust to their promises, how dangerous and full of anxiety to live at separate places

away from each other, among so faithless and mis-
chevious tribes, have resolved (upon the proposition and
promise made by the Director-General, the Honble
Petrus Stuyvesant, that he will give us a safe-guard
and further help and assist us in future emergencies) and
deemed it necessary for the greater safety of our wives
and children, to pull down our scattered habitations in
the most convenient manner immediately after signing
this agreement and to move close to each other to the
place indicated by the Honble General, to enclose
the place with Palisades of proper length with the assistance provided thereto by the Honble General, so that
we may protect ourselves and our property by such
means, to which the All-Good God may give His blessing, against a sudden attack of the savages; while we
bind ourselves, after imploring God and His divine blessing on all lawful means, to carry out directly, unami-
mously and without opposition the foregoing agreement
and to accomplish it as quick as possible under a penalty
of one thousand guilders to be paid for the benefit of the
settlement by him, who should hereafter make any
opposition by word or deed. To insure this still more,
we have signed this agreement with our own hands in
presence of the Honble Director-General and Sr
Goovert Loockermans on board the Ship 'Stede Amsterdam' in New Netherland. Done the last of May Ano
1658."
   It is signed.
"P. Stuyvesant

"Govert Loockerman   "Jacob Jansen Stoll
                      "Thomas Chambers
                      "Cornelis Barentsen Slecht
                      "Willem Jansen
                      "Pieter Dircksen
                      "Jan Jansen
                      "Jan Broersen
                      "Dirck Hendricksen Graaff
                      "Jan Lootman"

The place selected by Stuyvesant was staked out in the afternoon.

The Rondout Creek forms the southerly, the Hudson River the easterly boundary of the City of Kingston. From near the water's edge the hills rise quite precipitously to the height of from 150 to 200 feet. From the summit of the hills the land stretches away, a level plain, to the north and west. The City of Kingston was formed in 1872 by the incorporation of the two villages, Rondout and Kingston. Rondout being that portion of the city along the river, the Rondout Creek, up the hillsides and over a portion of the plain. The village of Kingston being the remainder of the plain. This plain or plateau on its northerly and easterly sides drops abruptly about fifty feet to the lowlands bordering the Esopus Creek about half a mile distant. On its westerly side the plateau also drops some distance to a ravine through which flows the Tannery Brook emptying into the Esopus Creek. This brook, in the olden days, must have been quite a stream, for a mill was erected upon it. The spot selected by Stuyvesant for the settlement was the northwesterly part of the plateau. It was quadrangular in shape having a circumference of about two hundred and ten rods. (A Dutch rod, 12 feet). If necessity required, it could be surrounded by water on three sides. The line of the stockade cannot be exactly located.

Approximately it began on the westerly edge of the plateau at about the junction of the present Green and North Front Streets; then ran along the northerly edge of the plateau, the present North Front Street, to about the present junction of that street with Clinton Avenue; then along the easterly edge of the plateau, the present Clinton Avenue, to the junction of that avenue with Main Street; then along the southerly side of the plateau, the present Main Street, to the junction of that street with Green Street; then along the westerly edge of the plateau along the Tannery Brook, along

Green Street, to the junction of that street with North Front Street, the place of beginning.

In 1695, John Miller, an Episcopal clergyman, who had been a surveyor, made a visit to Kingston with governor Fletcher and made a map of the stockade as it then existed. This shows its location as above stated. At the time of the building of the stockade, the settlers were between sixty and seventy in number. They could muster thirty fighting men. They had over three hundred acres sown to grain. Here, as disclosed by the records, are the names of the settlers and of those who had received patents for lands up to and including the year 1658:

Thomas Chambers, Christopher Davids, Jacob Jansen Stoll or Hap, Harmen Jacobsen alias Bamboes, Jacob Andriesen, Pieter Dircksen, Hendrick Cornelissen, Andries van der Sluys, Cornelis Barentsen Slecht, Willem Jansen, Jan Jansen, Jan Broersen, Dirck Hendricksen Graaff, Jan Lootman, Johanna de Hulter, Juriaen Westphael, Jan Verbeck, Francis Pietersen, Marten Metselaer, Peter Wolphertsen, Pieter Cornelissen van der Veen, Augustyn Heermans, Jacob Neus.

The location of their dwellings before they removed to the site selected by Stuyvesant cannot be exactly fixed. They were on the low lands on each side of the Esopus Creek.

On June 1, 1658, Stuyvesant met the Indians, about fifty in number. Gravely, silently, under a great tree they stood. There were the chiefs. Old Preumaecker, Seweckenamo, Ankerop and that baldhead Kaelcop. There were the warriors. Circlets of turkey feathers adorned the head. A breech-clout of deerskin or duffel cloth they had purchased of the whites is fastened around the waist. A plaid sash of the same thrown over the right shoulder, drawn in a knot around the waist, extends below the knees. Dearskin moccasins. Hatchet in belt. Gun in hand.

There, squatting upon the ground, wrapt in their

blankets, carefully guarding the children, the old squaws with wondering eyes watch the white men.

And there, too, we may be sure, are the belles of the tribe, with their sharp black eyes glancing admiringly at the brilliantly clothed soldiers. They are decked out in all their finery. A coat of finely dressed skin or bright cloth, girth around the waist, the skirt decorated with wampum, extends to the ankles. The long black hair hangs in a braid down the back into which strings of wampum are twisted. A head band around the forehead is fastened behind in a beaus knot. Bracelets of wampum are twisted about the wrists and a necklace of the same around the throat.

There were the pioneers. Redheaded Tom Chambers, Stoll, van der Sluys, and the rest of them, scowling at their foes. And there, sword by his side, dressed in slashed hose fastened at the knee by a knotted scarf; a velvet jacket with slashed sleeves over a full puffed shirt, knee breeches, rosettes upon his shoes, standing firmly on his wooden leg with silver bands, is the governor of New Netherland, Petrus Stuyvesant.

Stuyvesant, speaking through Stoll, who acted as interpreter, told the Indians that they had asked the whites to come to Esopus. They did not own or desire to own a foot of land they did not pay for. No harm had been done to them since he had been governor. He asked them why they had killed the hogs and destroyed the property of the settlers. Why they had set fire to their houses, killed Jacobsen and continually threatened to kill them all. He had come to learn the truth. He did not desire to make war or punish the innocent if the murderer was delivered up and the house paid for. One of the chiefs replied that the Dutch sold the "boisson" (brandy) to his people which made them "cacheus" (drunk). That then the young men could not be controlled. It was a Neversink Indian who had committed the murder and he was now living near Haverstroo. The Indian who had fired the house had run away.

They had not harmed the whites. They did not intend to fight but could not control the young men. At this the anger of the govenor blazed up. If the young braves wanted to fight they could do it then and there. He would match them man with man, twenty against thirty or even forty. Now was the time for them to fight instead of injuring the farmers, their wives and children who could not fight. If they did not stop he would destroy their crops, kill all of them and capture their women and children. He did not want to do that but they must pay the owner for his house, surrender up the murderer if he again came among them and do no more evil in the future. The people were going to move together and live in one place. It would be best if they sold him all their land in that vicinity and moved inland. To all of this the Indians said they would consider it, and " as the day was sinking" the meeting broke up. Stuyvesant again met them. They said they were ashamed of what had happened, but more because their young men had not dared to accept his challenge to fight. They would harm no one in the future and gave the governor six or seven strings of wampum and he in return gave them "two coats and two pieces of duffel," and again asked them to sell him the land where the settlement was to be formed which they promised to do. On the fourth of June, they came to him and stated that they had agreed to give him the land on which the settlement was being made "to grease his feet" because of the long journey he had made to come to see them. In the future they would not harm the Dutch but would live like brothers. To which the governor replied that they would do the same if they kept their promises.

In the meantime the inhabitants and the soldiers had been constructing the stockade and digging the moat. On the 6th of June Stuyvesant, finding that he was out of gun powder and needed some plank for a guard house, sailed away to Fort Orange to procure them.

On the 12th he returned, bringing with him "160 hemlock boards, 100 five and six inch, iron pins and an anker of brandy for the people working at the Esopus, as none had been put aboard or sent to me nor had I any for my own private use."

He found everyone at work and two sides of the stockade completed. On Sunday, the 16th, he looked over the land not yet purchased "and found it suitable for fifty bouweries." He was so pleased with the Esopus that he set the carpenters at work getting out lumber to build him a barn, for he had long intended to begin the cultivation of his land there. On the 17th and the 18th the palisades on the north side were put up, which was harder work because it could not be made so straight as the others. A guard house, made of boards, twenty-three feet long and sixteen feet wide, was built in the northeast corner of the enclosure. The carpenters engaged by Mrs. de Hulter to remove her house, barns, and sheds and others to build a bridge over the kill began their work. The stockade was completed on the 20th. On the 21st and the 22nd the houses of Chambers and Stoll were torn down and removed to the stockade and the beams for their barns put up. On the 25th, leaving twenty-four soldiers under Sergeant Andries Lourensen as a guard, the governor and the rest of the troops sailed for New Amsterdam. All went down to the kill to see them off. Gave him a good bye cheer as he stood there, firmly on his wooden leg, on the stern of the yacht devoutedly saying:—"The Lord be praised for His mercy and blessings on the successful execution of a matter, which every almost approved, as being necessary and honorable to our nation."

Then they went back to their unfinished homes within the stockade. There was a merry time in Esopus that night, in which the anker of brandy played its part. But by and by the revels ceased. Sleep fell upon the settlement. Outside the stockade, wrapped in their blankets, were the Indians. What dreams came to them. Slowly the night stole along. The pioneers slept soundly that night. Not a sound was heard save now and then the howl of a wolf in the thicket and the occasional scream of a panther falling on the startled night wind like the cry of a human being lost and wandering in the forest, while the stars looked down upon the new made village in the land of the Esopus.

CHAPTER IV

GROWTH

THE summer of 1658 was a hard one on the farmers. The continual rain spoilt the crops. The "worm" destroyed the oats. A freshet carried away the bridge over the kill.

The work of erecting the houses went on but was delayed because some of the people over the creek had not yet moved their dwellings. Although the hatchet had been buried with all due solemnity the Indians continued troublesome. They killed the horses of Mrs. de Hulter, a mare of Stoll, and worse than all, stole the "duffels and shirts" of van der Sluys. Early in August over five hundred of them appeared about the settlement, but after a few days disappeared, to the great relief of the inhabitants.

On October 9, 1658, Stuyvesant left New Amsterdam with fifty men to ascertain if the Indians had kept their promises made at his visit in May. On the 15th he met several of the chiefs at the house of Chambers. He reiterated the charges made against them in May and accused them of the offences since committed. He demanded the land he had viewed in May, "suitable for fifty bouweries," in payment of the expense of erecting the fort and removing the dwellings of the settlers. They must pay Stoll fifty strings of wampum for his mare; one hundred strings to Jacob Neus for destroying his house; and forty strings to van der Sluys for his "shirts and duffels."

They said they would consult the other chiefs and give an answer the next day. On the morrow, after a long talk, they agreed that Mrs. de Hulter could have her land for the killing of her horses. They had given Stoll seventy strings of wampum for his mare. That as for the land, Kaelcop was absent and Poenap, their greatest land owner, was at Fort Orange, so they could not answer until the next day. In token of their good intentions they presented the governor with four beavers, one of which had been sent by the Southern Indians, requesting them not to make war on the Dutch. That the Minquaes had told them the Dutch measured powder by snuff-boxes but they would be glad if it were measured to them by the handful. Giving a string of wampum they asked for powder "to shoot deer with and trade them to the Dutch"; and another string asking that the soldiers should leave them in peace and not beat them.

They did not appear the next day, so Stuyvesant sent Stoll and Marten Metselaer (the mason) to them, who returned with the report that the chiefs had "made game of them," that they did not intend to make satisfaction, "as they considered what they had done of no consequence."

Stuyvesant left in disgust, leaving Ensign Dirck Smith in supreme command with twenty-five men to be added to the present garrison of twenty-five. The ensign was instructed to give out the countersign and keep everything in good order. With the assistance of the inhabitants he should at once secure the settlement, mount a guard at the two gates and the guard house day and night, allow no Indian to enter the inclosure without the permission of Stoll and Chambers. No hostile act should be committed against the Indians unless they were the aggressors and then only in defense. The plowing and sowing should be kept up only when a guard of twenty of twenty-five men could be given, all of the inhabitants must work together taking their arms with them.

MASSACRE OF INDIANS AT HOBOKEN.

On October 28, 1658, the chiefs met Stoll, Chambers and Ensign Smith. They told them that they gave Stuyvesant one-half of the large tract of land he desired. They pointed out the portion they intended to retain for themselves. That, as they had given so large a present, they hoped the soldiers would lay down their arms and live as good friends ought. It was not always their fault but also of these who sold them brandy. That Stuyvesant ought to make them some presents in return, as this was a custom with them, and a sign of peace. They were promised that this should be done either the next spring or in the fall. So they parted and once again peace reigned.

Stoll, Chambers and Ensign Smith wrote all this to Stuyvesant. They told him he ought to give the Indians some presents in return. "The proverb says, a child's hand is soon filled, your Honor could easily fill their hands, upon which they sincerely rely, and say as before, they will see thereby your Honor's good heart and be assured, that your Honor forgives them their misconduct and say, quits." Those worthy Dutchmen conclude their letter with this most important postscript:— "All this talking has been done with dry lips. Your Honor may imagine, how zealously we have set here with these kings, but we hope, your Honor will remember his servants and give us something good for our lungs, which we could apply ourselves, if we had it."

It was a fair, square deal. Those Indians gave the land on the promise that they should receive some presents in return. White men, your representatives' Governor, made that promise. You had better see that it is kept, Governor. Look out. Be careful. Do not lie to them. If you do they may take payment in the blood of those Dutchmen at Esopus.

All was quiet during the winter of 1658-9. The Indians had gone to their villages. Esopus lay under the snow. The creek was frozen over. The great trees groaned and creaked as the icy wind swept through their branches. The oxen waded slowly through the snow drifts hauling fire wood to the village. The logs blazed in the huge fireplaces, while the smoke floated up through the hole in the thatched roof. The hogs had been butchered and turned into salt pork, hams and sausage. Wild turkeys were plentiful. Bear and venison steak could be had for a gun shot. They were a good-natured, merry people. We may be sure many a good dinner was served, many a frolic held. At Christmas time Santa Claus did not forget the children in the Esopus. On Sunday divine service was held. Led by van de Sluys they sang the same hymns their fathers had sung in the land across the water. So the winter wore away and then came the spring and summer of 1659. A summer long to be remembered in the Esopus.

The settlers were early at work getting the seed sown. George Westphael fenced Stuyvesant's land, got the oats planted but the seed wheat came to late. The governor's oxen "drew well" and the plowing went merrily on. The farmers agreed to work together, each helping the other, so that a guard of soldiers could be given. Cornelis Slecht and William Jansen broke this agreement without giving notice to anyone.

The laborers, who earned high wages, refused to do guard duty, so this fell upon the shoulders of the few inhabitants. They wanted some kind of a court so that everybody "could be made to go along." They intended to build a redoubt of sods near the guard house. All this was written Stuyvesant. They requested him to send them "the little bell from Fort Orange," and a "drum." Montagnie desired some "muskets' feuses." Juriane Bestvaal some more cows, a dwelling house and a farm hand. Some more lots ought to be surveyed, as there were several people who would like to cultivate the land.

Stuyvesant was short of drums, so he immediately wrote to the directors of the company in Holland to send him a dozen.

The Indians were quiet, but each side was distrustful and suspicious of the other. Danger lurked in the air. The Indians were sullen. They murmured because they had not received the presents for their land. They believed they had been lied to. That the promise had been made to keep them quiet and then unexpectedly attack them. They complained that their corn pits had been robbed, some beaver skins taken and that Boertsen had beaten one of them and pointing a knife at his breast had threatened to kill him.

There were rumors that they intended to build a fort on the land they had given Stuyvesant. They were making bows and arrows day and night. Sergeant Lourissen was warned by a Mohawk "Amiros" to be on his guard because the Indians intended to attack them at harvest time. Claes de Ruyter was told not to settle in the Esopus because the savages intended to go to war. The chief Kaelcop told "Kit Davids" he had better move away from the strand. This same "Kit" continued "at his old tricks" of selling liquor to the Indians and telling them lies as to the intentions of the soldiers.

In September Stuyvesant sent additional troops under Ensign Dirck Smith with three light cannons. On September 4, 1659, a party of about ninety-six Indians appeared at the settlement. They declared that they had no intention to do any harm. They desired to live in peace. They did not like it that they could not use the path that formerly ran through the guard house grounds. That it was lucky that the soldiers had just beaten a Sachem for using the path, for if it had been the young warriors they would have fought for it. They gave wampum for a horse and some hogs they had killed and asked that the Dutch should pay those who had done work for them. They were told that it would all be arranged when the governor came.

August 17, 1659, was a gala day in Esopus. On Stuyvesant's visit in 1658 he had promised the people that their request for a minister of the gospel should be complied with. This promise was kept much better than those made the Indians.

At his request the Classis of Amsterdam sent over the Rev. Hermannus Blom. He and dominie Megapolensis of New Amsterdam came to Esopus, and on Sunday, the 17th of August, Blom preached two sermons. So well did the people like him that on the very same day they "called" him to become their pastor. On the afternoon of that day Megapolensis had an interview with the Indians. They told him they had no evil intentions toward the whites. There was no truth in such reports. They had patiently borne the blows given them. They had quietly suffered four of their corn heaps to be taken. They showed seventeen staves of wood by which they signified that they had been wrongfully beaten that number of times. They were willing to keep the peace. They would prefer to submit to many things but they expected Stuyvesant would keep his promises as to the presents, for so long as that was not done they would think the general did not intend to remain at peace. The only reply the good dominie could make was that Stuyvesant was sick. As soon as he was well he would visit them.

On the 17th of September, 1659, Jacob Jansen Stoll sent Stuyvesant six bushels of seed wheat and asked him to send him "a piece of good linen for shirts." He says:—"What regards the savages, they are very quiet, but we do not know, what intentions the Almighty has concerning us."

Yes, they are quiet. Perhaps they will remain so *if* those presents come and *if* you keep the "boisson" from their lips. You had better do it Stoll. There is danger in the air.

CHAPTER V
THE WAR OF 1659-1660

IT was autumn in the Esopus. The summer was dying. The grain had all been gathered. The corn cut and shocked. Now and then a breeze, sweeping down from the mountains, foretold the colder blasts that were to come. The air, hazy and tremulous, wrapped valley and mountain in a thin, transparent curtain of gold. The mill stream and the creek ran drowsily as if ready for their winter's sleep. The birds were winging their way southward. The first light frosts had touched the wild flowers and the leaves. Every tree was a rainbow of color. The Catskills glowed with splendor never laid on canvas. All was quiet in the Esopus. It was September 20, 1659. Eight Indians had been husking corn for Thomas Chambers. Toward evening, their work done, they said to Chambers, "Come, give us brandy now." "When it is dark," replied Chambers. When the shadows fell he gave them a large bottle of brandy. Those savages, with courtly grace responded, "We thank you, that you have given us so much brandy." They went a little way from the fort, built a fire, squatted about it and drank. Around and around the circle went the bottle. About midnight the brandy was gone and they were very drunk. Like their white brethren, when in the same condition, they began to yell and make a great noise. They wanted another drink. Just one more. A nightcap. So they took account of their stock and found they had some wampum left. One of them went to Chamber's house and asked him for more brandy. He told him he had given them all he had. The Indian then staggered up to one of the soldiers and asked him if he had any brandy. He said he had. "Here is wampum, give me brandy for it." The soldier contemptuously answered: "No, what is wampum, what shall I do with it. Where is your kettle?" "I have no kettle but I have a bottle under my cloak," replied the Indian. The soldier filled the bottle for nothing. That Indian was grateful and said, "I am very much obliged to you."

Back to his comrades he went. They were lying on the ground crying, maudlin drunk. "Why do you cry, I have brought brandy?" he said. At that they began to laugh and clap their hands. Around went the bottle. Then a fight started. At this two of the eight left. Around went the bottle. One of them fired off his gun charged with powder only. It was ten or eleven o'clock. The yells of the Indians, the noise of the gun, had alarmed those in the fort.

Ensign Smith ordered Sergeant Lourissen to take nine or ten men, to go out one gate of the fort, return by the other and see what was the matter. He was ordered not to fight or molest anyone. In a little while one of the soldiers returned and reported that the commotion was caused by some Indians. Meanwhile, Jacob Jansen Stoll, although undressed to go to bed, appeared at the fort, gun in hand, followed by some of the inhabitants. The ensign ordered more men to go out. Stoll volunteered to accompany them and he, with Jacob Jansen van Stoutenburgh, Thomas Higgins, Gysbert Pjilipsen Van Velthuysen, Evert Pels, Jan Artsen and Berent Hermansen left the fort with the soldiers. The Indians lay about their camp fire in a drunken stupor. Suddenly one of them staggered to his feet. He was not quite as drunk as the others. He stood as if listening. Turning to the others he said:—"Come let us go away, I feel it in my body that we shall all be killed." They laughed at him and replied:—"You are crazy, who would kill us? We would not kill the Dutch, we have done them no harm, why, then, should they kill us and we have nothing to fear from other Indians?" "Yes," said the other, "that is true, but I am nevertheless so heavy hearted. Come, let us go, we shall surely be killed, may it come from whatever side it pleases, my heart is full of fears." Then he went off, hid his goods, and came back for one more drink. Ah, that last drink, for just then they heard the bushes crackle. They started to run. Too late. The white men were there. Crack went the guns. A sheet of flame lit up the darkness. One Indian was shot in the head. Another captured. At one poor wretch they fired continually, nearly taking his clothes from the body. They tried to take him prisoner. Drunk as he was, all the courage of his race came back to him: "Come, kill me, I am not afraid," he defiantly shouted and bounded away in the bushes. By the fire lay another, asleep, dead drunk. They cut him in the head with a sword. He jumped up, ran away a little distance "and the Dutch then ran back to the fort" and reported that the Indians had fired first.

There was no justification for this dastardly deed. It was a cold blooded murder. Stuyvesant wrote to the directors of the company in Holland that the trouble in Esopus was "the result of the inconsiderate action committed the night before against some drunken savages." It was investigated by the council at New Amsterdam. Its secretary, Cornelis van Ruyven, said that the whites were to blame. They had broken their promises to live with the Indians like brothers; and that the attack was without "any lawful reason." The Mohawk chiefs unanimously reported that the Dutch were to blame.

Jeremias van Rensselaer, writing from Rensselaerswyck to his brother, speaking of the war that followed, says, "It was commenced in a wholly disorderly manner, and the Dutch are most to blame, for they first shot an Indian."

After reading all the evidence, the directors of the West India Company in Holland declared, "Our people did court and begin this conflict."

Ensign Smith was very angry that his order not to fight or molest anyone had been disobeyed. He knew the consequences of what had been done. It meant war to the knife. He had already received orders from

Stuyvesant to come to New Amsterdam with eighteen of his men. He told the excited people that he would leave in the morning. They implored him not to desert them. In order to prevent his departure Chambers and Jansen hired the only available yacht and sent it up the river. Smith then determined to send a messenger down the river in a canoe to inform Stuyvesant of what had occurred. The next morning, September 21, 1659, Sergeant Lourissen with eight soldiers accompanied by some of the inhabitants, the whole party numbering seventeen or eighteen able bodied men, went down to the river to see the messenger off.

The news of what had occurred had spread among the Indians. They had already taken up the hatchet to avenge their slaughtered brother. On the return of the party they were surrounded by a large body of Indians. Jacob Jansen Stoll was mortally wounded. Lewies, the Frenchman, was killed. Resistance was useless. Thirteen in all, including the sergeant, surrendered and were carried off prisoners. Here are their names. Sergeant Andries Lourissen, Thomas Chambers, a son of Evert Pels, Abraham Vosburgh, Jacob Jansen Stoll, Pieter Hillebrant, Abraham Pieterze, William Carpenter, Pieter Lamertzen, Pieter de Buer, Pieter Dircks and his "man," a carpenter, by name Abraham.

Stoll died from his wounds in October. Chambers was exchanged for an Indian prisoner. Pieter Hillebrant and Pieter Lamertzen were returned by the Indians in November, 1659. Sergeant Lourissen either escaped or was ransomed, for he returned to Holland in 1660. The others, except Pels, were killed. It is said that some were burned at the stake. Pels married an Indian girl. He would not leave her and remained with her tribe. All honor to you, young Pels. All honor to you for not deserting your Indian bride and your unborn child. You half redeemed the fame of your father in taking part in the murder that led to your captivity. War now waged. Between five hundred and six hundred Indians attacked the village. The inhabitants did not dare leave the stockade. During the day the Indians lay concealed behind the trees and bushes. If one of the besieged chanced to expose himself a bullet whistled near him or an arrow buried itself in the logs of the stockade. Two were wounded and one killed. The nights were made hideous by the war whoops of the Indians. All night long one burning arrow after another shot up in the air like a rocket and fell within the stockade. The house of Jacob Hap (Stoll) took fire and was burned to the ground. The buildings outside the stockade were destroyed. The horses and cattle killed. It was only the foresight of Stuyvesant in building the stockade that saved the lives of the people. The attack continued for over three weeks. Then the Indians gave up hope of capturing the village and, their ammunition exhausted, they disappeared. News of the attack on Esopus reached Stuyvesant on the 22nd or 23rd of September. The report quickly spread.

The farmers living in the outlying settlements, fearing another Indian uprising, began fleeing to Manhattan. Stuyvesant, though sick, rode about among the people and succeeded in allaying the panic. He assembled the Burgomasters, Schepen and the captains of the train bands and told them of the conditions of affairs at Esopus. The people there must have relief which could only be given by the citizens of Manhattan. They replied that in their opinion, "by beating the drum," volunteers could be obtained if the savages who might be captured were declared prizes.

For two days rat-a-tat, rat-a-tat, rat-a-tat sounded the drums in the crooked streets of New Amsterdam. Only six or eight recruits were obtained Terror had seized the people. Some declared, "that they were bound only to defend their own place, that no citizen could be compelled to place his body and life in danger against barbarous savages."

Nothing daunted Stuyvesant who drafted the workmen from his farms and even the clerks in his office. To these he added six soldiers from New Haerlem and three from Staten Island and so got together a company of thirty-six men. The cowardice of the people stirred the wrath of the governor. On the 3rd of October, the three companies of citizens were assembled under arms. There, quaking with fear, they stood facing the irate governor. He told them of the attack on Esopus. Even while he was speaking their brethern might be butchered by the savages. What was their duty. Where was their honor. Under like circumstances they would expect relief and assistance. Let those who were not cowards step forward and join the officers and train men of the companies. Even this fervid appeal did not stir the people. Not more than twenty-five volunteered to go. This not being enough one of the companies was drafted by lot and ordered to be ready to sail the next Sunday under a penalty of fifty guilders. If any were faint-hearted or afraid he might find a substitute or be free upon payment of the fine.

On Sunday the company of citizens, numbering about one hundred, with the office clerks and trainmen and twenty-four or twenty-six Englishmen accompanied by about as many friendly Indians from Long Island boarded the yachts. As this motley army was embarking a dog on shore began to bark. The sentries, alarmed, fired their guns at an imaginary foe. Consternation reigned. The Indians were coming. Some of those gallant Dutchmen on board the boats, wild with terror, leaped overboard into the water like so many frogs, swam to the shore and disappeared in the bushes. They set sail on Monday, October 6, 1659, and arrived at Esopus on the 10th. On reaching the settlement they found that the Indians had disappeared. A heavy rain had fallen causing a freshet in the creek whose waters covered the low lands nearly five feet in depth. Pursuit of the Indians was impossible. So after viewing the ruins of the buildings that had been burned and leaving a supply of powder, lead, medicine and other necessaries Stuyvesant and his army sailed back to Manhattan. The Mohawks had heard of the attack at Esopus. In October, 1659, two of their chiefs appeared before the council at Fort Orange and asked if the whites intended to make war on them. Then they visited the Esopus Indians and on November 1, they, accompanied by some of the Esopus chiefs, came to the settlement, bringing with them two of the captives, Pieter Lamertzen, a soldier, and Peter Hillebrant. A truce was signed to last for as long as it pleased Stuyvesant.

The winter of 1659-1660 passed without further trouble. Occasionally some of the Indians visited the settlement and traded deer and wild turkey for powder.

Each party distrusted the other. Stuyvesant wrote Ensign Smith to be on his guard. Not to allow any of the Indians further into the fort than the house of Thomas Chambers "between the palisades." If possible to capture some of them but not to do so unless it could be immediately followed up by an attack on their nearest village.

On the 9th of February, 1660, Stuyvesant delivered a message to his council and the burgomasters at New Amsterdam relating to the attack on Esopus. He referred to the Indian war of 1655 and called attention to the number of whites that had been killed by the Indians during his administration. Owing to the failure to punish them they had grown insolent. They believed the whites to be too weak to punish them. They thought one savage was the equal of two Dutchmen. Something must be done to restore the prestige of the Dutch. The land at Esopus was the most productive in the colony. The inhabitants there must be protected. He urged that war be declared against the Esopus Indians. That one hundred and forty or one hundred and fifty men be enlisted for that purpose. Councillors Nicasius de Sille and Cornelis van Ruyven replied in writing. The former agreed with Stuyvesant; van Ruyven opposed war. He maintained that the whites were to blame for the recent trouble. They had first attacked the Indians and had broken their promises that they would live with them like brothers. The condition of the colony would not warrant war. It would be better to make treaties with the Indians which, if they broke, war would be more justifiable. These opinions were read to the burgomasters. In February, after a long debate, it was resolved that war against the Esopus Indians was unavoidable but on account of the present weakness of the colony it should not be begun before fall, and in the meantime one hundred or more men be enlisted.

On March 25, 1660, a proclamation of war was issued. It warned every person to be on his guard against the Indians and directed all skippers not to sail on the North River except in company of at least two or three yachts manned with at least six men. On March 15, 1660, Coetheos, chief warrior of the Wappings, addressing the council at New Amsterdam, stated that he was sent by the chiefs of the Esopus who desired peace. The council replied that they were willing to make peace but they had been told that the Indians had said they would only make a mock peace and when the Dutch least expected it they would surprise and kill them. He replied that he had heard this but only the barebacks, the low or bad savages, said it, the chiefs wanted peace. He was finally told that if they desired peace they must come to New Amsterdam. If they did not dare come Stuyvesant would go to Esopus. In April, 1660, the chiefs of the Katskills at Fort Orange in behalf of the Esopus chiefs made proposals for a lasting peace. The Esopus Indians would surrender the whole Esopus and the lands on and along the kill and leave it. They would restore what they had taken from the whites, wampum, cloth, cutlasses, plows and other articles. They would surrender, against ransom, the Christian prisoners, reconcile them with wampum and the whites were to deliver up the Indian captives. At the same meeting the Mohicans and Katskill Indians for themselves requested that Stuyvesant make peace with the Esopus, and offered to make him a large present of wampum in token of their gratitude.

These propositions were communicated by the magistrates at Fort Orange to Ensign Smith at Esopus and to Stuyvesant. Afterward one of the Katskill chiefs visited Esopus and made the same offer to Ensign Smith who informed Stuyvesant of the same stating that the indians "call only for peace, peace and await your honor's mercy."

In May, 1660, Stuyvesant sent Claes de Ruyter to Esopus to negotiate with the Indians. He instructed him to endeavor to obtain an interview with them and inform them that they must come to New Amsterdam to sue for peace. Ensign Smith and de Ruyter failed to find the chiefs. The Indians evidently were afraid. In the same month three Mohican chiefs asked the council at New Amsterdam that peace be made. Presenting wampum they asked for the return of the Indian captives which was refused. The council inquired what they intended to do with the Christian captives, to which they made no answer. They asked that the war cease. To which the council replied that if the Esopus kept quiet the Dutch would do the same. As for themselves if they had nothing to do with the Esopus they would be treated as men and brothers. They were presented with three blankets, three pieces of duffel, six small kettles, three axes, three pair socks and each a pound of powder.

While these endeavors of the Indians to bring about a peace were going on a desultory war was being waged. In March, 1660, an attack was made on one of their villages, during which three or four of them were killed. Stuyvesant, who was then at Esopus, sent twelve prisoners to New Amsterdam.

In April, 1660, Ensign Smith with forty-five men lay in ambush for the Indians a short distance from the fort, but the Indians discovered them and fled. One was killed and one prisoner taken. Three of the whites had their horses killed under them.

On a May morning in 1660, Ensign Smith with seventy-five men marched up the Rondout Creek to raid an Indian village. The Indians disappeared in the woods. All but one. All but Preumaecker the oldest chief of the Esopus. There he stood confronting the officer and his seventy-five men. Let Ensign Smith describe the scene. "As he was a very old man and spoke arrogant words to our men, saying, 'what are you doing here, you dogs,' and aimed his gun at us, we took away his gun and six knives and a hatchet, and as it was a great distance we could not take him along and therefore gave him a whack with his own hatchet." A brave deed, O Ensign Smith. You already held his son captive. You had disarmed him. But he was a very old man, and it was a long distance back to Esopus so— you killed him. A dastardly deed, O Ensign Smith. You will hear of it once again when the toma-hawk spatters the brains of the men, women and children upon the ground and the flames of their homes light up the sky.

In June, 1660, Stuyvesant dispatched Claes de Ruyter to Esopus to receive the proposals of peace made by the Indians. He reported to Stuyvesant that they wished chiefs would meet him. Stuyvesant, accompanied by Marten Cregier and Oloff Stevenson van Cortland, left New Amsterdam for Esopus July 7, 1660, and arrived there on Sunday, the 11th, and here on July 15, 1660, a treaty of peace was made. It was a notable gathering. The chiefs of the Maquas, Mohicans, Kattskills, Minquas, Wappings, Hackinkesacky and Staten Island were there to urge the Esopus to enter into a treaty of peace and to stand sponsors for them that its terms would be kept.

Kaelcop, Seewackemano, Neskahewan and Paniyruways appear for their people of whom a large number were present.

The settlers were all there. Stuyvesant told the Indians that they had burned houses of the Dutch, attacked the village, killed the prisoners taken by them and stole the ransom that was ready for them. Nevertheless, he was willing to forgive all this, and at the solicitation of the other tribes make a lasting peace with them. The chief of the Maquas then addressed the Esopus. He said that the whole country was assembled on their account to solicit and conclude a peace for them. If a treaty was not made and they began war he and the other chiefs would not intercede for them. They must not kill any horses or cattle, nor steal anything, but they must buy or earn it and live with the Dutch like brothers. Addressing the settlers he admonished them that they should not begin war and should not box the ears of the Indians and then ridicule them. Taking a hatchet from one of the Esopus chiefs he threw it upon the ground and trampled it into the earth, saying:— "Now they shall not begin again for their lives" to which the Esopus chiefs responded, "Now we have let the hatchet be taken from us and trampled into the ground, we shall not take it up again in eternity."

The terms of the treaty were then discussed and agreed upon. In token of its acceptance Stuyvesant presented each of the Esopus chiefs with a "piece of cloth" and delivered them three of their number who had been taken prisoners. He gave each of the chiefs of the other tribes a piece of cloth. The treaty provided that all hostilities should cease, and all injuries forgotten and forgiven by either side.

The Esopus Indians promised to convey to Stuyvesant all the territory of the Esopus and remove to a distance from there, without ever returning again to plant. This tract of land was the low lands bordering the village and extending two or three miles on each side of the Esopus Creek.

They also promised to pay Stuyvesant in return for the ransom taken for the captured whites five hundred schepels of corn. They agreed to keep the treaty inviolable, not to kill any animals of the Dutch or if it should happen to be done the chiefs were to pay for it, and in case of their refusal one of them was to be kept a prisoner or under arrest until the loss was paid or made good. The Dutch were to do them no harm. If the Dutch should kill a savage or the savages a Dutchman war should not be immediately commenced on that account but complaint should be made and the murderers delivered up to be punished as they deserved. The Indians should not come armed to the Dutch farms or houses but might come and go and trade as before. As the last war was caused by drunken people no savage should be allowed to drink brandy or strong liquor in or near the Dutch settlements but must go with it to their land or to some distant place in the woods. The old annals quaintly state that the treaty was agreed upon "under the blue sky."

But a cloud hung on the horizon. It grew and expanded, black and portentous. In the years to come it blotted out the heavens and its folds were crimsoned by the flames roaring upward from the ruins of Wildwyck.

Only a few days before he left for Esopus to conclude the treaty, Stuyvesant had the Indian prisoners held by him transported to Curacao, an island of the Dutch in the Caribbean Sea. Sent these free sons of the forest to toil as slaves under the burning sun of the tropics. Two of them were afterward returned and the others promised that if they behaved well they would be released.

The Indians never forgot and never forgave it. It was in revenge for this, more than for any other reason, that they laid Wildwyck in ashes in 1663.

Stuyvesant owned land at Esopus from which he derived considerable revenue. The rich meadows bordering the Esopus Creek were the most productive in the colony. There was no forest. They were ready for the plow. Stuyvesant tried to obtain them from the Indians in 1658 but failed. He and the settlers at Esopus looked upon them with covetous eyes. The attacks of the whites upon the Indians; the repeated refusal of Stuyvesant to listen to any proposals for peace unless the chiefs came to New Amsterdam; and the declaration of war were prompted more by a desire to obtain these fertile fields for nothing than by a desire to punish the Indians for wrongs committed by them. The boast of some of the historians of New Netherland that all the lands acquired from the Indians were paid for is not true so far as Esopus is concerned.

Several causes lay at the bottom of all the trouble between the whites and the Indians. To the Dutch the red men were but savages. They stood in their way. They had no rights which they were bound to respect. They were outside the pale of justice and of law. To kill one was no crime. The Dutch failed to keep the promises made them, stole their property, beat them, and generally treated them with derision and contempt. The Indians were certain to avenge such acts as the deliberate killing of the old chief, Preumaecker, and the murder of their drunken brethren at Esopus. Nearly every injury done to the whites by the Indians was in retaliation for offences against them by the Dutch. Still those Dutchmen were no worse than other men of that day. No worse than the men of this day and generation. The same story has been written whenever and wherever the civilized man confronts the uncivilized.

The root of all the trouble was the traffic in intoxicating liquor carried on with them by the Dutch. When the red man was himself he was quiet, inclined to peace, well satisfied with a piece of gay cloth, a trinket, an axe, or a little powder. When brandy took possession of him he became, as his white brother became, a maudlin, reeling fool, a stupid, ugly brute, or a demon incarnate. Every one recognized the evil. The council at New

Amsterdam characterized it as "very dangerous, injurious and damnable." Law after law was enacted prohibiting the giving or sale of liquor to the Indians, but still the traffic went on, and would go on, so long as a Dutchman could "sell a pint of brandy for a schepel of wheat." But those Dutchmen paid for it. Paid for it with the ashes of their homes and the blood of their kindred.

CHAPTER VI

WILDWYCK AND THE NIEU DORP

DURING the years 1661 and 1662 life in the village ebbed peaceably along. Its quiet was unbroken save by an occasional row between some of its contentious citizens. The Indians made no disturbance. In May, 1661, grants of land were made, by lot, to Hendrick Hartensen, Harmen Hendrick, Jan Jansen from Amesfoort, Jacob Barentsen, Jan Lootman, Jacob Joosten, Willem Jansen, Pieter van Haelen, Matthys Roeleffs, Jan Willemse, Anthony Creupel, and Gerret Jansen van Campen.

The inhabitants of Esopus were ordered to have their land surveyed by the sworn surveyor within six months. Have it marked and divided by proper signs and, upon certificate of the survey, were to receive a deed for it.

The settlement had grown in numbers and importance. The time had arrived when some form of government should be established. On the 16th of May, 1661, Stuyvesant issued the following order erecting the settlement into a village:

"Peter Stuyvesant, Governor and Director-General, commissioned and authorized in the control of all matters relating to the public good of all the territories of New Netherland, by virtue of the authority and permission of the Honorable Lords, the Directors of the Privileged West India Company, Greeting:—The aforesaid valiant Director-General, Peter Stuyvesant, observing the situation and condition of the place called 'Esopus' already inhabited six or seven years, and pleased thereat, hath, in consideration of its state and population, erected our place into a village, and honored it with the name of Wildwyck by which name it shall hereafter be called."

In the records the name Wildwyck is variously spelled Wildwyck, Wiltwyck, Wildtwyck, Wildwijck. The letters "ij" of the Dutch in names have usually been transcribed as "y" in English. While Swartwout kept the Wildwyck records he wrote the word "Wildtwyck" afterward the more scholarly Capito, "Wildwyck" and I have followed his spelling. Wilt is an old spelling of Wild meaning "wild," "savage." The final "d" in Dutch words is not pronounced as in English like a soft "d" but hard like "t" so that the singular of "wilden" "savages" in Dutch records is written "wilt" instead of "wild." "Wyck" is an old form for modern "wijk" and means "retreat," "refuge," "quarter." The authorities differ as to the meaning of the word. Some give it as "A village or fort, a refuge from the savages." "Wilt" also means "game" and therefore others give it the meaning as "a place where game is abundant," as Beaverwyck means a place where beavers are plenty.

May 5, 1661, a court was established by order of Stuyvesant and his council. He appointed Evert Pels, Cornelis Barentsen Sleght and Elbert Heymans Rose, schepens of judges.

The jurisdiction, power and authority of the court will be hereafter given. It held its first session July 12, 1661. Roeloff Swartwout was appointed Schout. His duties combined those of our district attorney and sheriff.

Swartwout had a hard time getting his job. He was appointed by the directors of the West India Company, April 15, 1660, and a commission, defining his powers and duties, issued to him. He was to remain in office for four years after which the office would be abolished unless the directors might before abolish it or extend the time. On his arrival at New Amsterdam Stuyvesant would have none of him. He wrote the directors of the company that he was very much astonished at his appointment because of his minority and his unfitness for the place. His appointment was premature, as there was no court at Esopus and it did not appear that there would be one for a long while for want of inhabitants "fit to sit on the bench." When the time came a man of greater age, capacity, and esteem would be required.

The directors replied that they were astonished at Stuyvesant's objections. Their judgment was sufficient in the matter. He was old enough to be fit. If he was deficient in that respect he had time enough to outgrow it. They wished their orders strictly obeyed. Although the doughty old governor did not like it he thought it better to obey the orders of the company and so commissioned Swartwout sheriff, May 23, 1661. In November, 1661, Stuyvesant promulgated several ordinances regulating the affairs of the village.

No person should perform any work at his ordinary business on Sunday, whether plowing, winnowing, transporting wood, hay, straw or grain, threshing, grinding or conveying any goods to or from the strand, on the penalty of one pound Flemish ($2.40) for the first offense, double as much for the second and four times double as much for the third. No one should give entertainment in taverns, or sell or give away beer, wine or any strong drink on Sunday under the above fine. If any person was found drunk on Sunday he was fined one pound Flemish, for the benefit of the officer, and be confined in the watch house during the pleasure of the court. In order to prevent fires no person should construct any plastered or wooden chimneys or kindle any fire in houses with walls or gables made of straw, or in the center on the floors of other houses covered with thatch unless there be a good, solid plank ceiling in the house.

The court should appoint two fire wardens. They

should every fourteen days or three weeks inspect all houses and chimneys and see that they were properly constructed and cleaned. The negligent should be fined as above mentioned.

In order to prevent damage to the cornfields by horses, cattle and hogs everyone must keep tight his fences and gates. A pound, in which the animals doing damage were to be restained was ordered erected. The owner of the animals should be fined for the damage done. Every person must fence his lot within four months and build on the same within one year, without selling or conveying to others, in default of which the court must grant the lot to others "who are better disposed and more industrious." As the stockade had begun to decay and openings had been made in the same which remained unclosed during the night, "to the imminent danger of the place and advantage of the enemy" the sergeant was commanded to repair it. All openings must be closed at night. If anyone did not close and shut at night what he had opened during the day he should be fined for the first offense three guilders, for the second double as much and for the third two pounds Flemish.

Dominie Blom took charge of the congregation at Wildwyck in September, 1660. In 1661 a parsonage was erected. In order to pay its cost the court, on November 12, 1661, was by order of Stuyvesant directed to "levy and collect from every morgen (2 acres) of land whether of pasture or tillage land, which anyone about the aforesaid village occupies or claims as his own, one Rix dollar (a little over $1.00) per morgen, beaver value, in good wheat, payable one half down and the other half, without fail, next summer and, further, from the other inhabitants who possess only lots and no lands according to their means."

The following were the persons assessed and the amounts expressed in guilders:

Jurriaen Westvael, tenant on Balthasaer Lasar
  Stuyvesant's bouwery, 25 morgens.......... 62.10

The Hon. Director-General for a point 12 morgens.. 30.00
Jurriaen Westvael, for his land, 28 morgens...... 70.00
Thomas Chambers, 2 bouweries, each 40 morgens 200.00
Evert Pels, his bouwery, 30 morgens.......... 90.00
Albert Heymans, on the bouwery of Jacob Jansen,
  Stoll's widow, 30 morgens.................. 90.00
Roeloff Swartwout, tenant on the bouwery of
  Jacob Jansen Stoll's widow, 43 morgens...... 107.10
Cornelis Barentsen Slecht, tenant on the bouwery
  of Mrs. d'Hulter, 64 morgens................ 160.00
Cornelis Barentsen Slecht's own claimed land for
  which he has neither survey nor patent esti-
  mated at 25 morgens 62.10
Mrs. de Hulter's unsurveyed pasture land, esti-
  mated at 25 morgens 62.10
Albert Gysbert's land, 20 morgens............. 50.00
Aert Jacob's land, 47 morgens................. 117.10
Tjerck Glaessen's land, 50 morgens............ 125.00
Aert Pietersen Tack, 20 morgens.............. 40.00
Michiel Foure, 4 morgens.................... 10.00
  The following house lots of those who have no farm
lands:
Andries van der Sluys, lot................... 10.00
Jan Aerts, smith, voluntarily offers........... 20.00
Michiel Fouree 12.00
Jan Broese 10.00
Jan the Brabander........................... 10.00
Andries Baerents 12.00
Hendrick Cornelisse assessed................. 20.00
Hendrick Jochemse, offers................... 20.00
Harmen Hendrick 12.00
Jan Jansen, carpenter, assessed............... 10.00
Jacob Barents, offers........................ 12.00
Jacob Joosten, offers........................ 12.00
Pieter van Aelen, assessed................... 10.00
Matthys Roelofse, offers..................... 15.00
Jacob Burhamse, offers...................... 20.00
Gerrit van Campen........................... 10.00

Anthony Greupel 10.00
Albert Gerrits 10.00
Baerent Gerrits 25.00
Jacob Blanson 10.00
Jan de Backer offers 1000 bricks.
Willem Jansen 12.00

The amount realized from the foregoing tax not being sufficient to cover the cost of the parsonage Stuyvesant, on November 21, 1661, by ordinance directed the court for the term of one year to levy and collect an excise tax of four guilders from every tun of strong beer; sixteen guilders from a hogshead of French wine; six guilders from each anker of Spanish wine; brandy or distilled liquors and all larger and smaller casks in proportion. Each inhabitant of the village must make a return of the liquors in his dwelling or brew house and pay the excise to Jacob Burhamse, the collector; the same to be paid in heavy money, twelve white and six black wampum beads for one stiver. No person should remove or transfer any liquor until a return of the same was made and tax paid on forfeiture of the liquors, and five times its value to be applied, one-third to the officer, one-third to the informer and one-third to the church.

The names of those who paid the tax and the sum paid, expressed in guilders (a guilder 40 cents), are as follows:

Hendrick Jochems...75- 7
Pieter Hillebrantz... 2
Aelbert Gyssbertz....12
Jacob Burhams......71-14
Gerret Forcken......12
Walraeff du Mont...24
Jan Barentz Timmer-
    man 1
Barent Gerritzen....65
Gritiez Westerkamps 1
Jan J a n s e n Bra-
    bander 14
Jan Lambertz....... 3

Lewis Dubo.........11
Jan Barentz Snyder...14
Michiel Verbruggen.. 1
Jan Pierssen........12
Wouter Aelbertz.....24
Thomas Swartwout...12
Pieter van Halen..... 6
De jonge Gesellen..... 2
Theunis Voocht....... 1
C o r n e l i s Barentz
    Slecht 70-7
Arent Jacobs........ 4
Aelbert Heimans......55

Joannes Leblem..... 2	Mathies Capito....... 4
Dirck Ariaens....... 1	Hendrick Cornelissen. 3
Jan Barentz Backer. 6	Dom. Herm. Blom....58
Juriaen Westphalen..33	Matthiees Roeloffs....16
Michiel Verre....... 3	Jan van Bremen...... 4
Gertruyd Andriessen.14	Jan Aertsen Smit.....17
Cornelis Jansen,	Wilm. Jansen........12
sawyer 13	Dirck Wilmssen...... 9
Picter Bruyn........ 2	Thomas Chambertz...84
Evert Pelsen........40	Schout Swartwout....32
Hendrick Hendrix... 4	Pieter Martensen..... 2
Claes Pietersen...... 2	Pieter Jellissen....... 2
Sergeant Christiaen.23	Jonas Rantzoo........ 5
Andries Barentz..... 9- 7	Cornelis Brantz....... 2
Ariaen Huyberts..... 1	Tjarck Glaessen...... 8
Maryken Huygen.... 6	Kerst Kerstensen..... 2
Pieter, the miller.... 2	Gerrit van Campen... 2
Bart Siebrantz.......22	Hendrick Jansen Loo-
Huybrecht Bruyn.... 3	man 20
Arent Pietersen Tack 6	Matthies Princen..... 2
Wilm. Jansen Stoll... 4	Jan du Parcq......... 2
Wilm. van Vreden-	Marten Harmsen.....17
borg 16	Matthies Blancian....51
Gyssbert Gyssbert-	
zen 52	

A total of 1111.15 guilders, a little over $444.

On November 22, 1661, the court, Stuyvesant being present, adopted an ordinance that a new road be opened from the village to the new and undivided lands. The same "shall pass over the land of Evert Pels along the side of the kill and over across the land where it is narrowest, over Jacob Jansen Stol's land, thence in a straight line through the great lot away unto the Dwars Kill."

In order that the cornfields might not be damaged by animals running at large on the road the same should be travelled only with wagons or horses under bridle or in traces. Loose cattle or foals beside the mares should not be driven over the road under penalty of one pound Flemish for each animal so driven. A swing gate should be erected at the beginning of the road and always kept closed by a person appointed by the court for that purpose. He should receive for opening and closing the gate such sum as the owners of the farms should agree upon. From others and those with whom he could not agree he should receive one stiver for each opening, two stivers for each freight or pleasure wagon and one stiver for each person therein. Some of those taxed for the building of the parsonage failed to pay. The salary of dominie Blom was in arrears. There was a short crop of grain. Not sufficient for the garrison. For these reasons Stuyvesant, on November 24, 1661, issued an ordinance that no grain was to be exported after the freezing up of the river until his further order. The corporal at the Redoubt, on the Rondout creek, was directed to permit no liquor to enter from the river without his permit, showing the quantity, quality, and to whom consigned, in order that it might be entered with the collector and the excise paid. Complaint having been made to Stuyvesant that unstamped grain measures were used by reason of which the quantity of grain delivered fell short of the legal measure, he, on November 27, 1662, issued an ordinance forbidding the use of any but legally stamped measures under a penalty of twenty-five guilders.

On the same day all persons were forbidden from receiving any articles in pawn from the soldiers at the garrison, under a penalty of twenty-five guilders for the benefit of the garrison and in addition of restoring the pledged articles without the redemption money.

Nearly all the buildings in the village had thatched roofs of reeds or straw. The people were in the habit of burning straw and other refuse in the streets, thus exposing the buildings to damage or destruction by fire. On October 16, 1662, it was enacted that no person should set fire to any refuse within the village. The same must be carried a musket-shot outside the stockade to posts to be erected by the court. Any person failing to do so was to be fined for the first offense, fifty guilders, for the second one hundred guilders and the third time to be arbitrarily punished as an example to others.

The dangerous practice was continued as late as 1664, for on November 14, of that year, the court ordered that all straw and rubbish should be carted across the mill dam.

Each person must clean the street in front of his own lot within four days, under a penalty of ten guilders.

It appearing in November, 1662, that openings had again been made in the stockade the same were ordered to be closed within twice twenty-four hours with palisades or proper doors with locks, provided the key be returned every night to the guard house. Every person offending was to be fined one pound Flemish. March 6, 1663, the court ordered that the owners of private meadows near cultivated lands should fence the same. The wolves caused great damage to domestic animals.

October 9, 1663, the court offered a bounty of twelve guilders for every male and eighteen guilders for every female wolf, payable in wampum, killed. The wolf must be taken to the schout for inspection. Every farmer was required to contribute one guilder in wampum to pay the bounty. In June, 1662, Juriaen Teunissen petitioned Stuyvesant for leave to keep a tavern at the mouth of the kill, at the north side of it, where his foster father, Kit Davitsen, formerly lived. His request was denied because it "would tend to debauch the soldiers and other inhabitants and it is also feared that strong liquor might be sold there to the savages."

In the same month Sergeant Christian Niessen applied for an increase in pay, saying that his present salary was not enough to live on. He was allowed twenty guilders per month. The rich valley of the Esopus was known to the residents about Fort Orange. In April,

1662, Philipp Pietersen Schuyler, Volckert Jansen (Douw) and Goosen Gerritsen van Schaick, of Beverwyck, presented their petition to the council at New Amsterdam. Van Schaick came from Westerbroeck, province of Utrecht. In 1637 and for some years after he worked upon one of the manor farms at Rensselaerswyck. He served as a member of the court at Beverwyck from 1648 to 1651. In 1659 he was engaged in tanning. After 1660 he is occasionally referred to as Gerritsz van Schaick.

Schuyler came from Amsterdam in 1650. He married Margareta van Slicktenhorst, daughter of the director of Rensselaerswyck and resided there. They had ten children of whom, Peter, was the first mayor of Albany. His grandson was General Philip Schuyler of Revolutionary fame.

Volckert Hanz, after 1651, usually referred to as Volckert Janz and Volckert Janz Douw, is first mentioned as working at Rensselaerswyck in 1647. He was a farmer and a trader. The petitioners stated that as the prosperity of the province rested principally upon agriculture and commerce they desired to establish a new village at the Great Esopus, "where a great deal of uncultivated land lies." They asked that a survey for a new village be made and that it be laid out in lots. That forty or fifty morgens of land be granted them. They promised to immediately enter upon the same, cultivate and build houses and barns on the same. April 6, 1662, the council resolved to lay out a new settlement and to accommodate the petitioners as occasion should permit. The place selected for the Nieu Dorp (new village) was the rich bottom lands bordering the Esopus creek, about three miles west of Wildwyck. The English governor, Lovelace, named the village "Hurley" in honor of his family. The Lovelace's being barons of Hurley, Ireland. In 1663 grants of land at the new village were made to the petitioners Jansen, Schuyler and van Schaick, and also to Anthony Crepel (Crispell),

Cornelis Wynkoop, Louis DuBois, Roeloff Swartwout, Hendrick Cornelisse van Holsteyn Lambert Huyberts (Brink) and Jan Tomassen. Others leased lands usually for the period of four years. The leases provided that the lessees should have the land rent free for the first year, after that at the annual rent of four hundred and fifty guilders in beavers at eight guilders, or in grain at the market price, beaver valuation, calculating a beaver at sixteen guilders. They should cultivate the land and erect buildings which, at the end of the term, should belong to the lessor. The lessor was to furnish one hundred boards for a house, the use of three mares, one gelding, a young stallion, two cows, two heifers, two sows with pigs, six hens and a rooster, a plow, a cart with all things belonging to it, except a plow chain. One-half the natural increase of the animals belonged to the lessor. Many of the lessees purchased the land at the expiration of their lease.

March 30, 1663, Stuyvesant issued an ordinance that all persons claiming land at Wildwyck, or in the new village, must apply for and receive deeds for the same within two months.

They must also begin to cultivate and fence the same or forfeit the land. All persons who had applied for or received lots in the new village must fence them within six months or forfeit the lots and a fine of twenty-five guilders. Albert Heymans Roose, Jan Joosten and Jan Gerrets were appointed overseers to see that the work was done and the fines exacted.

April, 1663, the proprietors of land at the new village petitioned the council at New Amsterdam that each might be granted a lot for a garden in the low land on the kill. They also asked that they be allowed to pass free and unmolested through Wildwyck to and from the strand.

The records of Wildwyck contain two papers of great interest. One is a list of the persons to whom lots had been granted prior to 1661 and during that year and

1662. The other shows the financial condition of the village. They are here given entire.

Old Lots

No.
1. Thomas Chambers.
2. Evert Pels.
3. Balthazar Laser Stuyvesant.
4. Preachers house and lot.
5. Mrs. de Hulter.
6. Jacob Haps' little bouwery.
7. Jacob Haps' second bouwery.

8. Henry Zeewant ryger.
9. Andries the weaver.
10. Jan Brabanter.
11. Jan Brouwersen.
12. Michiel the first.
13. Michiel Verre.
14. Jan the smith.
15. Andries van der Sluys.
16. House and lot of Gertrey Hansen lying opposite to Nos. 6 and 7.

New Lots

No.
1. Hendrick Jochemsen.
2. Hendrick Martensen.
3. Harmen Hendricksen.
4. Jan Jansen Timmerman.
5. Jacob Barentsen.
6. Jan de Backer.
7. Jacob Joosten.
8. Willem Jansen.
9. Pieter van Alen.
10. Matthys Roeloffsen.
11. Jacob Beerhans.
12. Gerrit van Campen.
13. Anthony Crupel.
14. Albert Gerretsen.
15. Meerten Gysbert.

16. Dirck Adriaen.
17. Matthys Capito.
18. Jan Lammersen.
19. Carsten de Noorman.
20. Barent Gerretsen.
21. The Church Yard.
22. Jan Barensen.
23.
24. Alert Heymansen.
25. Juriaen Westvael.
26. Nicolaes Willem Stuyvesant.
27. Albert Gysbertsen.
28. Tjerick Glaesen.
29. Aert Jacobsen.
30. Jan Schoon.
31. Aert Pietersen Tach.

"Revenue and Expenditure of the Village of Wildwyck, including the Building of the Ministers House.

Income of Wildwyck Village.

From 525 morgens.

The land pays fl 2.10 st. per morgen in general,

which computed gives a total of......fl 1312.10   coin
The house lots, not paying land tax,
have
    In wampum 272.fl
    In coin ....136.
    In coin ....   136.

The excise on wine and beer, farmed
out, has fetched so far, that is to the
21st of November, 1662..............   1003.18
    In wampum 1505.17

    In coin 669. 5. 6
The revenue is altogether...........   2117.16. 6
Remains a balance of...............   889.11.10
      The Outlays for the Ministers House.
Bricks, tiles, lime, boards, wainscoting,
slating, iron, hinges, locks and nails, and
everything required for it
    In wampum 680.50
    In coin 953.13
    All reduced to coin.................   1293.15.8
Paid for wages of the carpenters and
masons, hod carrier, for freight of bricks,
tiles, boards to this place
    In wampum 1387.5
    In coin .... 570.
    Reduced to coin...................   1263.12.8
Board for the carpenters, masons and hod
carrier altogether
    In coin ....   450.
Total in wampum.............fl 2067.10
Total in coin.................   1973.13
The wampum reduced and added to the
coin makes it..........................   fl 3007.8
    "Besides the above there must be paid to the Court
Messenger for the making and keeping in repair of the
gates, to Juriaen Westvael for hire of the house of

Domine Blom, who lived in his upper room, 80 florins."
New-Year's day, 1663, was ushered in with a parade of
the trainband. Very brave and formidable they looked
marching through the snowy streets. At the open door
of every house stood mother and the children. The little
ones, afraid at the unusual sight, clung tight to her
ample skirts. The boys ran along with the troops, pelt-
ing each other with snowballs as they ran. Through the
little streets, around the stockade, they marched, trying
to keep step with the drum that had come from over the
sea, while the colors of Holland kissed the frosty air.
Here and there stood an Indian, silently, gravely, looking on. No smile rested upon their lips. Not a word
did they utter. Only the dark eyes flashed and the
fingers tightened around the gun-barrel as they thought
of their brethern toiling in slavery in a far away land.

After the parade the Citizen's Council of War adopted
and posted up an ordinance regulating the conduct of the
troops. Each one appearing for training without proper
side and hand-arms, powder and lead, should, for the
first time, be fined twelve guilders; for the second time
double that sum; and the third time according to the
judgment of the court-martial. Each one absent or
coming late was to be fined two guilders, sergeants, cor-
porals, and lancepesades double that sum. In case of an
alarm of fire the members of the captain's squad were
to assemble at Barent Gerretsen's, the brandy distiller;
the lieutenants squad near Albert Gysbertsen's, the
wheelwright; and the third squad at Hendrick Jochemsen's. No one should appear while intoxicated. Any
one swearing or profaning God's holy name and sacra-
ments should be fined twenty-five guilders. The magistrates thinking that these regulations infringed upon
their prerogative of enacting ordinances tore down the
same which does not seem to have caused any bad blood
between the parties.

The day ended with an entertainment given the
soldiers by some of the villagers. What a feast they

must have had. Lucullus would have given his villa at
Tusculum to have been present. Supawn. Wild turkey;
a saddle of venison; roast pig and fried rolletje. Pota-
toes mashed and in their jackets. Onions, squash and
cole-slaw. Hazel, hickory and butternuts. Apple and
pumpkin pie. Crullers and oly-koeks. Hard cider, beer,
and an anker of brandy from Gerretsen's distillery. All
the prominent citizens were there. Tom Chamber,
Tjerck Glaessen de Witt, Evert Pels, Alaert Heymans,
Roose, Sergeant Christiaen Nissen, Schout Swartwout,
and above and beyond all, Dominie Blom. In the huge
fire place the logs sputtered, cracked, and burst into
flame, roaring ever high and higher as the hickory sticks
were piled on the blaze. Every man of them had pipe
and tobacco. The fragrant smoke filled the room, swaying, trembling, floating up through the great chimney.
The mugs of beer and brandy were never empty. Every
one of them, including the dominie, was trying to drink
his neighbor under the table. At gibe, and jest and joke
their loud honest laughter shook the building. Out upon
the night air floated the songs of father land. The eyes
of men who had undaunted faced death in an hundred
shapes grew misty with tears as they thought of the old
home so far away. But by and by the revels ceased.
Back to their homes they went. Some of them singing,
swaying, as they tramped through the snow. The
silence of the night fell upon the village. In each home
the lights were put out. The back log in the fire place
banked in ashes. The old folks went to bed. The lover
and his sweetheart, locked in each others arms, bundled
beneath the same blanket and—methinks—above them,
an angel hovered, smiling, his finger upon his lips.

No disturbance broke the peace of the village during
the winter. Then spring came and the farmers were
early at work in the fields preparing the land for the
seed. The Indians had been quiet, very quiet. Still
doubt and mistrust hung in the air. The sale of brandy
to them continued. It was certain to breed trouble. The

INDIANS BRINGING TRIBUTE.

traffic was carried on at the new village. The magistrates wrote Stuyvesant that they had found half an anker of "distilled water" at the house of Loweys Dubo (Louis DuBois), a Walloon which had not been reported. They confiscated it "because some mischief might result from it," and asked that an order be made that the residents of the new village should pay the excise to the collector, Jacob Boorhans, at Wildwyck, "for the liquor distilled here is not to the taste of the savages which is for the advantage of the savages and to the loss of the country."

The presents which had been promised the Indians for the land at the new village had not been made. Early in April, 1663, Stuyvesant was warned that if this were not done at once trouble would ensue. But above and beyond all the captives whom Stuyvesant had banished to the far off isle of Curacao had not been returned. This the red men would not forget or forgive. The fires of hate and revenge smouldered. Soon they would burst into flame.

CHAPTER VII.

THE WAR OF 1663

IT was Thursday, the 7th of June, 1663. Away off in the distance the peaks of the Catskills pierce the blue of the sky. On the low lands the wheat is softly swaying in the breeze, a shimmering sea of green. The brook, just below the stockade, laughs and gurgles on its way to the creek and the river. The air is redolent with the perfume of spring. The corn fields are ready for the plow. The children are at play in the streets. The women about their household work. Albert Gysbertsen and Tjerck de Wit are near the mill gate. Schout Swartwout with some men at work near his house. Dominie Blom with two carpenters are at work on the parsonage. Chambers just outside the stockade. A soldier or two lounged near the guard house. Most of the men were away at work in the fields. It is between eleven and twelve o'clock in the forenoon. Several small bands of Indians sauntered through the gates almost unnoticed. Nearly four years had passed since the last trouble. The peace had not been broken.

The hatchet remained buried in the earth. No one thought of danger. Through the streets strolled the Indians, offering corn and beans for sale. They chattered with the women and laughed at the children at play. Suddenly a horseman dashed through the mill gate, shouting as he rode, "The Indians have destroyed the new village." Instantly the dread war whoop of the red men was heard. Then a scream, wild and piercing, the scream of a woman rang out. An Indian had snatched the little girl of Jan Albert's and buried his hatchet in her head. Crack, crack went the guns. Fire, some one shouted. A house on the south side of the village burst into flame. The wind was blowing from that direction. The Indians had fired the village. In a moment pandemonium reigned. Another house caught fire. Then another and another. The smoke rolled in red billows through the streets. The sparks fell in showers. The flames roared upward. The shrieks of the women and the wail of the children never ceased. Above it all rang out the wild yells of the Indians as they ran through the streets, slaughtering as they went. Through the palisades rushed Chambers. "Lock the gates." "Clear the gun," he shouted. In a few moments the handful of men turned on the Indians. It was too late. They were already outside the stockade driving the women and children before them. Mothers clasped their babes in their arms, shrieking, crying as they were forced along. On, on to the woods the Indians drove them. Their piteous wails floated back ever faint and fainter until the forest shut them from the sight of the helpless men in the village. The wind changed to the west. This was all that saved the village from being entirely consumed. The men began to return from the fields. What a scene of desolation greeted them. The homes of many were burned. The dead lay in the streets. The half burned bodies of wife and child smoked in the hot ashes of their homes. Well did Dominie Blom say:—"I am he who hath seen misery in the day of the wrath of the Lord. O my Bowels—my Bowels. I am pained at my very heart, and with Jeremiah, O that my head were water, and mine eyes a fountain of tears, that I might weep for the slain of my people; for the dead lay as sheaves behind the mower."

Here is the record of that day, written many, many years ago. No pen can give a more graphic picture.

"List of the Soldiers and Settlers, killed, wounded, or taken prisoners by the Indians at Wildwyck, on the 7th of June, 1663."

MEN

Barent Gerretsen, murdered in front of his house.

Jan Alberts, murdered in his house.

Lichten Dirrick, murdered on the farm.

Willem Jansen Seba, murdered before his door.

Willem Jansen Hap, murdered in Pieter van Hael's house.

Jan the Smith, murdered in his house.

Hendrick Jansen Looman, murdered on the farm.

Thomas Chamber's negro, murdered on the farm.

Hey Olferts, murdered in the gunner's house.

SOLDIERS

Hendrick Martensen, on the farm.

Dominicus, in Jan Alberts' house.

Christiaen Andriessen, on the street.

WOMEN

Lichten Dirrecks' wife burnt, with her lost fruit, behind Barent Gerretsen's house.

Mattys Capito's wife killed and burnt in the house.

Jan Albertsen's wife, big with child, killed in front of her house.

Pieter van Hael's wife shot and burnt in her house.

CHILDREN

Jan Alberts' little girl murdered with her mother.

Willem Hap's child burned alive in the house.

TAKEN PRISONERS

Master Gysbert's wife. (She was the wife of Gysbert van Imbroach, a surgeon, and the daughter of La Montagne, vice director at Fort Orange.)

Hester Douwe.

Sara, the daughter of Hester Douwe.

Grietje, Dominie Lacr's wife. (The wife of a Luthern dominie.)

Femmetje, sister of Hilletje, being recently married to Joost Ariaens.

Children

Tjerck Claessen de Witt's oldest daughter.

Dominie Laer's child.

Ariaen Gerritsen's daughter.

Two little boys of Mattys Roeloffsen.

KILLED IN THE NEW VILLAGE

Marten Harmensen found dead and stript naked behind the wagon.

Jacques Tyseen beside Barent's house.

Derrick Ariaensen shot in his house.

TAKEN PRISONERS

Men

Jan Gerritsen on Volckert's bouwery.

	Women	Children
Of Lowis du Bois	1	3
Of Mattheu Blanchan	1	2
Of Antoni Crupel	1	1
Of Lambert Huybertsen	1	3
Of Marten Harmensen	1	4
Of Jan Joosten	1	2
Of Barent Harmensen	1	1
Of Grietje Westercamp	1	3
Of Jan Barents	1	1
Of Michiel Ferre	.	2

Of Hendrick Jochems 1
Of Hendrick Martensen 1
Of Albert Heymans 2

Women-Children 8 26

HOUSES BURNT IN WILDWYCK

Of Michiel Ferre...... 1	Of Hans Carolusen....	1
Of Willem Hap........ 1	Of Pieter van Hael....	1
Of Mattys Roeloffsen.. 1	Of Jacob Boerhans....	2
Of Albert Gerretsen... 1	Of Barent Gerretsen...	2
Of Lichten Dirrick..... 1	Of Mattys	1

Houses 12

The new village is entirely destroyed, except a new uncovered barn, one rick and a little stack of reed.

WOUNDED IN WILDWYCK

Thomas Chambers, shot in the woods.

Henderick Jochemsen, shot in his house.

Michiel Ferre, shot in front of his house. (Died of his wounds June 16, 1663.)

Albert Gerretsen, shot in front of his house.

Andries Barents, shot in front of his house.

Jan du Parck, shot in the house of Aert Pietersen Tack.

Henderick, the Heer Director General's servant, in the street in front of Aert Jacobsen.

Paulus the Noorman, in the street."

It will be observed from the above that most of the persons taken prisoners came from the new village. (Hurley.)

News of the massacre reached Stuyvesant on June 12, 1663. He sent a letter to the surrounding towns informing them of the event and cautioning them to be on their guard.

On the 14th he was at Wildwyck. Christiaen Niessen, the commander of the militia; Thomas Chambers, the captain of the train band; Hendrick Jochemsen, the

lieutenant; Swartwout, the Schout; and Albert Gysbertsen, Tjrick Cleassen de Witt, Gysbert van Imbrogh,
the magistrates, were appointed a council to take charge
of all matters. The people were commanded to obey
its orders. Matheus Capito was appointed secretary.
The council at New Amsterdam convened on June 17 to
consider the condition of affairs at Wildwyck. To at
once attack the Indians would be perilous. They would
at once kill the captives. To ransom them would be very
costly and the Indians would not consent unless a treaty
of peace was made, only to be again broken. It was
finally resolved not to make peace, but to try to get the
Mohawks and Senecas to effect the release of the
prisoners. In the meantime the relatives of the captives
were to be urged to ransom them without the knowledge
of the council, for which purpose they would be assisted
with merchandise for presents to the Indians.

Johan de Decker, one of the council, was sent to Fort
Orange to obtain assistance. He was instructed to get
the magistrates there to induce the Mohawks to procure
the prisoners without ransom and without any engage-
ment for a treaty of peace. If this could not be done to
capture some of the Esopus Indians, to be used in exchange. He was to ascertain if volunteers for an attack
upon the Indians could be obtained and was authorized
to engage to pay them eight or ten guilders per month
at the usual rate of sixteen pieces of wampum per stiver
and furnish them with weapons. He was also to
negotiate a loan with the merchants of three thousand
or four thousand guilders, half in goods and half in
wampum, for which the governor and council would give
as security not only the company's but their private
property.

Decker did not meet with much success. The Senecas
were at war with the Minquas. The settlers were panic
stricken at the news from Wildwyck and flocked to the
fort for protection. All was in confusion and nothing
could be done.

At last an Indian, "Smiths Jan," accompanied by several Mohawks and "Jan Dirck," a Dutchman, were prevailed upon to visit the Esopus Indians.

These Mohawks reached the fort of the Indians. One of them by a present of a piece of wampum got one of the Esopus chiefs, who had Mrs. van Imbroch in charge, to promise to deliver her to him in the morning. But at dawn the Esopus and his captive had gone. The other chiefs offered to return the wampum which the Mohawks indignantly refused, saying that if they had their arms with them they would take the woman by force. The party returned to Wildwyck and reported that the Indians cared not so much for the captured savages as for payment for the land taken for the New Village, if that were done they would release the prisoners. In the meantime Mrs. van Imbroch had escaped and returned to Wildwyck. Mrs. van Imbroch reported that the fort of the Esopus in which she and the other captives were kept was about eight hours' march south of Wildwyck. It was at the foot of a hill to which it leaned at one side. On the other side the land was flat.

A creek, not deep, and which could be easily crossed washed one corner. There were two rows of palisades and a third was being erected. The fort had two gates, one to the north and the other to the south. About thirty men were in the fort. They manifested great anxiety concerning their women and children and lodged them with the prisoners outside the fort during the night.

On June 25th Stuyvesant issued a call for volunteers for an attack on the Esopus Indians. They were offered "free plundering and all the barbarians who are captured." For the term of one year they were to be exempt from guardmounting, firewatch and chimney tax. The owners of bouweries were exempt from tithes for six years and those having no bouweries to have the same exemption when they established bouweries in addition to the ten years commonly allowed. Those wounded were to be properly treated by the surgeon.

For the loss of the right arm they would receive eight hundred florins, for the left arm five hundred florins, for the loss of a leg four hundred and fifty florins, for the loss of both legs eight hundred florins, for the loss of an eye three hundred florins, for both eyes nine hundred florins, for the loss of the right hand six hundred florins, for the left hand four hundred florins, and for both hands one thousand florins.

Volunteers came in slowly. Only five or six from the English villages on Long Island and nine from Bergen. On June 30, Marten Kregier, one of the Burgomasters of New Amsterdam, was commissioned commander of the force to be sent to Wildwyck. He, with Nicolas Stillewel, Pieter Wolphertsen van Couwehoven and Sergeant Christian Niessen were constituted a council of war and to them was committed the conduct of the same.

Cregier arrived at Wildwyck July 4, 1663. Things were in bad shape. The people were disheartened. Fearing another attack they had shipped most of their cattle, over one hundred head, to Fort Orange. The soldiers had received their last ration. Food was scarce. There were not over one hundred men capable of bearing arms. Nine of the Negroes were wounded and six were at the Redoubt on the river. According to report the Esopus Indians, together with a few Wappingers and Manissings who had joined them, numbered about two hundred. A band of these had crossed to the east side of the river and lay concealed back of Magdalen Island (near Tivoli). Cregier dispatched some soldiers against them. A skirmish took place in which five Indians were killed. Among the number was Veldoverste, an Esopus chief. They cut off his hand and brought it back with them, together with a squaw and three children they captured. But one soldier was killed and one "bitten by a rattle snake." It was learned from the squaw that the Esopus were about eighty strong and a number of Manissings had joined them. Their fort stood on the brow of a hill, was quadrangular in shape, and defended by three rows of palisades. The dwellings within were encircled by thick cleft palisades with port holes and covered with bark. At night the prisoners were kept in the woods. On July 9 additional troops under Lieutenants van Couwenhoven and Stillewel arrived. On the 16th three of the Mohawks who had come down from Fort Orange with "Smiths Jan" were sent to the Indian fort to negotiate for a return of the prisoners. They took with them one of the captured Indian children and sixty-three guilders in wampum for ransom. They obtained the release of five prisoners, two women and three children, who were freely given, on their promise to return three of the prisoners held by the whites. The fort had been abandoned, the Indians scattered among the hills, the prisoners distributed among them. They again returned to the fort, taking with them the squaw and two children. This time they succeeded in securing the release of but one captive, a woman. The Indians refused to release any more unless Corlaer and Rentslaer came to the fort with goods for ransom and a peace was concluded, which must be done in ten days.

Cregier seems to have had considerable trouble with the people of the village. They did not manifest a lively disposition to assist him. Some refused to furnish teams and wagons to bring up supplies from the river. "Some refused to work for the company; some gave for answer if another will cart I also shall cart; some said, my horses are poor, I cannot cart; others said, my horses have sore backs, and other such frivolous answers." Tjerck Classen de Wit, although a magistrate, threatened to turn some soldiers out of a small house they occupied. He said he had hired it, although he neither had possession "nor procuration for it." Cregier told him that the soldiers would be removed on condition that he, "as a magistrate, would have them billetted in other houses as the men could not lie under the blue sky, and as they had been sent here by the chief government for the defense of the settlers. But he made no answer to this and so there are other ring-leaders and refractory people in this place."

While Cregier and the magistrates were examining the Wappinger Indians at the house of Chambers as to the whereabouts of the Esopus Albert Heymans Roose (Roosa) and Jan Hendrickensen appeared at the door and threatened to shoot the Indians. Cregier told them they must not do it. To which they replied, "We will do it though you stand by." "I told them in return to go home and keep quiet or I should send such disturbers to the Manhattans. They then retorted I might do what I pleased, they would shoot the savages to the ground, even though they should hang for it." Roosa, nothing daunted, came into the room and told the magistrates that one of them should step out. Cregier naively adds, "What his intention with him was I can't say." To our mind it is very clear. Albert was a fighter. He thought he could lick the entire court, at least one of its members.

It was now determined to attack the Indian fort. The expedition, led by Cregier, started from Wildwyck on the morning of July 26, 1663. It consisted of ninety-one men of Cregier's company and thirty from Lieutenant Stillewel's. Lieutenant van Couwenhoven commanded forty-one Indians from Long Island. There were six volunteers from Manhattan. Thirty-five men from Wildwyck, of whom eleven were horsemen. There were seven of the company's Negroes. Each had one pound of powder, one pound of ball, two pounds of hard bread, one-half a soft loaf, two pounds pork and one-half a Dutch cheese. This left at Wildwyck thirty-six soldiers and twenty-five freemen. By evening they were "two great miles" from Wildwyck. Here they bivouacked, not being able to get through the woods at night. The next morning the march was resumed. The trail they followed ran through an unbroken wilderness. Trees had to be felled to make bridges over swamps and streams. The hills were so steep that the wagon and cannon had to be hauled up by ropes. On reaching the fort in the evening they found it abandoned. The Indians had fled. A squaw, cutting corn, was captured. On the 28th, a detachment of one hundred and forty men were sent to the mountain where Mrs. Imbroch, who had been taken along as a guide, had been held prisoner. No Indians were to be seen. The captured squaw pointed out another mountain about two miles away to which she said the Indians had fled with seven prisoners. Again the troops pushed on through the forest, only to be again disappointed. Their foes had gone. The squaw, being again asked if she did not know where the Indians were, pointed out another mountain, but there was no path and the troops were compelled to return. On the 28th and 29th all hands were engaged in cutting down the fields of growing corn surrounding the fort. Over two hundred and fifteen acres were destroyed and over one hundred pits full of corn and beans were burned. On the 31st the fort and all the wigwams were set afire. Were the red men watching? What would be their answer to the destruction of their homes? For a little, the troops stood looking at the blaze roaring upward; then at the word of command, they began the march back to Wild-wyck, which they reached about nine o'clock in the evening. The course from Wildwyck to the fort was mostly southwest about ten miles. Various locations have been assigned for the fort. From all the data it is probable that it stood on what is known as Indian Hill, in the village of Warwarsing, about twenty-two miles southwest from Kingston on the homestead property of the late John C. Hoorbeek, deceased.

The Indians still lurked in the woods about the village. To venture forth without protection was dangerous. On August 4th, the Council of War adopted an ordinance forbidding either large or small parties to leave the village without the consent of the Captain

Lieutenant and only under proper convoy of soldiers. To stop the waste of powder and ball, every one unnecessarily discharging any firearm was to be fined three guilders for each shot. The court was kept quite busy imposing fines upon persons who violated these ordinances. The soldiers would get drunk even on Sunday. Every member of the militia was, by ordinance, forbidden from selling or pawning the goods advanced to him for liquor. All those engaged in selling strong drink were prohibited from receiving such property for liquor and from furnishing drinks on Sunday.

During the month of August the farmers were busily engaged in getting in the grain. A great rain interfered with the harvest and carried away several of the palisades of the fort.

Some of the Esopus were hiding with the Wappinger Indians just north of Newburgh. Lieutenant van Couwenhoven sailed down the river and secured the release of four of the captives, a woman and three children. He brought two of the Wappingers. They reported that they had been with the Esopus where they were building a new fort about four hours from the fort that had been destroyed. Cregier determined to attack it with a force of one hundred and twenty men. The magistrates of the village were requested to furnish twenty horsemen from the hired men of the village to accompany the soldiers, and some horses to be used in bringing back the wounded. "After great trouble they obtained six horses from a few, but spiteful and insulting words from many. One said, let those furnish horses who commenced the war, another said, I'll give 'em the Devil—if they want anything they will have to take it by force. The third said, I must first have my horse valued and have security for it; and so forth, with much other foul and unbecoming language, not to be repeated." Thomas Chambers, without solicitation, gave two horses.

With one of the Wappinger Indians as a guide, and

Christoffel Davids as interpreter, Cregier and his force left Wildwyck September 3, 1663, at one o'clock in the afternoon, and marched three miles to the creek, "which runs past the Redoubt." Here they passed the night. It rained very hard. The creek was high, the current very swift. They got across by holding on to a rope they had thrown across the stream. After a march of about four miles they camped for the night. They set out at daybreak on the morning of the 5th, and about noon came to the first corn field of the Indians, where they saw two squaws and a Dutchwoman who had come from the fort to gather corn. About two o'clock in the afternoon they came within sight of the fort. It was situated on a lofty plain. It was not as large as the one previously destroyed. It was a perfect square with one row of palisades set all around, being about fifteen feet above and three feet under ground. Two angles of stout palisades, as thick as a man's body, having two rows of portholes, one above the other, had been completed and the Indians were busy at the third angle. When near the fort, the attacking party was seen by a squaw who at once let forth a terrible scream. "The Indians rushed forthwith through the fort towards their houses, which stood about a stone's throw from the fort, in order to secure their arms, and thus hastily picked up a few guns and bows and arrows, but we were so hot at their heels that they were forced to leave many of them behind. We kept up a sharp fire on them and pursued them so closely that they leaped into the creek which ran in front of the lower part of their maize land. On reaching the opposite side of the hill, they courageously returned our fire, which we sent back, so that we were obliged to send a party across to dislodge them. In this attack the Indians lost their chief, named Papequanaehen, fourteen other warriors, four women and three children, whom we saw lying on this and on the other side of the creek, but probably many more were wounded when rushing from the fort to the houses, when we did give them a brave charge. On our side, three were killed and six wounded and we have recovered three and twenty Christian prisoners out of their hands. We have also taken thirteen of them prisoners, both men and women, besides an old man who accompanied us about half an hour, but would go no further. We took him aside and gave him his last meal. A captive Indian child died on the way, so that there remained eleven of them still our prisoners." It was necessary to get the wounded home as soon as possible, for which reason the growing corn was allowed to stand for the present. The wigwams contained a considerable quantity of bear and deer skins, blankets, elk hides, guns, powder and belts and strings of wampum. Placing the wounded upon horses, one upon a litter, loaded with booty, accompanied by their prisoners and the rescued captives, the little army took up the march back to Wildwyck, which they safely reached September 7th at about noon. An additional force of forty Marsepingh Indians arrived under van Couwenhoven. On October 1st, Cregier and his troops started for the scene of their late victory. The fort was deserted. Not an Indian was seen. The dead braves had been thrown into large pits. These the wolves had rooted up and devoured some of the bodies. The corn was pulled up and thrown into the creek. The fort and wigwams tore down, piled in a heap and burned to ashes. The fort was about twelve miles from Wildwyck on a course of South, Southwest. The way was very bad and hilly. Several large creeks had to be crossed. In some places there was very fine land.

The fort destroyed was situated in the town of Shawangunk, about four miles west of Wallkill village, just above the Shawangunk Creek. The property is now (1917) owned by Antonia Blaustein. A detachment of troops was .sent to Sagers Killetie (Saw Creek) in the present town of Saugerties, about twelve miles north of Kingston to destroy some corn fields of the Indians. They reported that it was beautiful maize land, suitable for a number of bouweries and for the immediate reception of the plow. September 25, an awful tragedy happened. "A soldier, Jurien Jansen, fell out of a canoe at the Redoubt and was drowned; he was reaching for a squirrel and the canoe thus upset and he was drowned." Demon rum still held sway. Some of the villagers got so drunk "that they cannot distinguish even the door of the house." Fights and brawls disturbed the peace. Something must be done. So, on September 26th, the "valiant Council of War" directed Schout Swartwout "to notify and forbid the tappers and retailers of strong drink who follow the profession of selling liquor in this village, that they do not under present circumstances sell strong drink to any one, be he Christian or Indian, under forfeiture of the liquor that may be found in his house."

October 7th, a girl who had been held captive by an Indian at his hut in the mountain on the other side of the creek, escaped and returned to the village. On the 9th, forty of the militia and the Marseping Indians (from Long Island), who had fought with the whites, went back to Manhattan. They took with them the captured Esopus. On the 17th, another detachment of the soldiers returned, leaving about sixty at Wildwyck under the command of Ensign Niessen.

The stockade was in need of repair. The Court ordered that each farmer should set up new palisades in front of his lot. The others, being inhabitants or burghers, occupying thirty-nine lots in the village, should repair and place new palisades "from the water gate along the curtains unto the lot of Arent Pietersen Tack." They must be at least two feet in circumference and thirteen feet in length. Every person must appear on Monday, October 22, at 7 o'clock "at the gate near Hendrick Jochemsen's, to proceed with the work."

November 7th, Lieutenant van Couwenhoven returned

from Manhattan, bringing with him two children captives whom he had exchanged with the Esopus for a
squaw and a big girl. Eight of the Indians captured
at the new fort were sent back with him. He was
accompanied by a Wappinger chief, who offered to
return home and bring back one of the captive women
who was among the Wappingers. He kept his promise
and was given in exchange an Esopus squaw and child
and two pieces of cloth. He said he would do his best
to get all the prisoners held by the Esopus within ten
days.

On November 29th he was back again, bringing six
of the captives with him. For these he was given
a captive squaw and two children, thirty strings of
wampum, one piece of cloth, two cans of brandy, one-
half an anker of brandy, fifteen strings of wampum,
three yards of duffel, and ten pounds of powder. He
said that he had given wampum to another Indian to
look up the child of Albert Heymans (Roosa) and would
bring all the other prisoners within three days. He
returned on December 2nd, having two children with
him, for which he was given an Indian child and three
pieces of cloth. He could not return the remaining
captives, five in number, because they were at the hunting grounds of the Esopus and he could not find them,
but he had an Indian looking for them. Two were in
his vicinity. The squaw who kept them would not let
them go because she was sick, had no children and
expected to die when he would get them and Roosa's
daughter, who was also at the hunting grounds.

On the last day of the year, December 31, 1663, Cregier, his work well done, sailed away for Manhattan.

During December, 1663, the chiefs of the Hacking-
kesaky and Staten Island Indians appeared before the
council at Manhattan. They stated that Seweckenamo,
one of the chiefs of the Esopus, was anxious for peace.
He was ashamed to come himself because he could not
bring with him the five remaining captives. He could

not get them because they were with the Esopus at their hunting grounds. He promised to get them as soon as possible. The Council concluded a truce with the Esopus for two months, during which the captives must be returned.

On March 6, 1664, the child of Jan Lootman was returned, and on the 25th, the chief of the Wappingers brought back another child. He said there were only three more captives among the Esopus. On April 26, 1664, Stuyvesant wrote the directors of the company that they had got back all the captives but three and his proclamation of May 31st, designating June 4 as a day of thanksgiving for the return of the captives, states that all of them had been returned. Legend has it that one of them, the daughter of Berent Slecht, married a young brave called "Jan." They settled on the bank of the Esopus Creek in the present town of Marbletown, where they lived for many years. Her name is not among the list of captives. Some of these prisoners were in the hands of the Indians for nearly a year. They were held by "savages," by "barbarians" panting for revenge upon the white man. All but one were women and children. Not one of them was sent away into slavery. Not one was killed. Not one was injured. The honor of no woman was assailed. All were returned. A most remarkable fact to reflect upon when forming our estimate of the nature of the red man.

On May 15, 1664, a notable gathering assembled in the council room at New Amsterdam. His "Noble Worship the Director-General Petrus Stuyvesant presided. About him were the Hon. Nicasius de Sille, the Hon. C. V. Ruyven, the Hon. Cornelis Steenwyck, the Hon. Paulus Leenderstsen van der Grist, Burgomasters of the city, Captain Lieutenant Marten Cregier, Lieutenant van Couwenhoven, Govert Loockermans, of Staten Island; Thomas Chambers, Commissary of the village of Wildwyck; Jacob Backer, President of the Schepens, and

Abraham Wilmerdonk. Sara Kierstede acted as interpreter. There, gazing proudly at the white men, stood the chiefs of many of the tribes of the red men. Seweckenamo, Onagotin and Powsawwagh of the Esopus. t'Sees-Sagh-gauw of the Wappingers. Meeght Sewakes of the Kightewangh. See-Segh-Hout of the Reweuhnongh of Haverstraw. Sauwenarocque of the Wiechquaskeck. Oratamy of the Hackingkesacky and Tappaen. Matteno of the Staten Island and Nayack. Siejpekenouw, brother of Tapusagh of the Marsepingh, with twenty warriors of his tribe.

Old Seweckenamo, holding a stick in his hand, his arms folded, said: I have asked my God Dachtamo that I may do some good here. Let a treaty be made here as solid as this stick. The chiefs here are well pleased that peace be made between my people and the Dutch. It shall include the Marsepingh. I come to ask for peace for my people. A peace as firm and as binding as my folded arms. The other chiefs of the Esopus cannot be here. One is a very old man and blind. The others are friends of mine. I speak for them.

After much talk the terms of the peace was agreed upon. The treaty provided that all that had happened should be forgiven and forgotten. All the land that had previously been given to the Dutch and that which they had taken in the late war as far as the two captured forts should remain the property of the Dutch. The Indians should not plant this land again nor come into the villages at Esopus. In order that they might not be entirely deprived of their land they might during this year plant around the old and new fort. No Indian should come upon land which the Dutch were cultivating or using for pasture. They might come to the Redoubt to sell their corn. They must not come with more than two or three canoes at once and must send a flag of truce ahead to tell that they were coming. For their accommodation a house should be built over the hill. If a Dutchman should kill an Indian or an Indian a

Dutchman war should not be immediately begun. A meeting should be first held over it and the murderer punished by death in the presence of the Indians and the Dutch. If the Indians should happen to kill any of the live stock of the Dutch the chiefs should pay for it. If they refused one of them should be kept in prison until the animal killed was paid for. No Dutchman should do any damage to the Indians.

This treaty marks the passing of the Indian. He was no longer a menace or a terror. The Esopus were scattered among the other tribes. Their forts and villages had been burned. Their corn fields destroyed. Once again, in July, 1664, Seweckenamo appeared at Manhattan. He told the council that his people were sick and "very lean" for want of food. He asked that provisions be sent to them to their country "on the other side of Haverstraw." He was told that it would be better for them to come to Manhattan for supplies, but they could purchase provisions of the whites in their country. They gave him some wampum and a piece of duffels. In return he presented several strings of wampum and an elk skin and then, sadly, proudly, strode from the council chamber. On May 6, 1664, Dominie Blom and his consistory sent a petition to Stuyvesant asking that June 7th of every year be designated as an anniversary or thanksgiving day, on which no work should be done, to commemorate the rescue of the captives and to "thank his Divine Majesty for it." The pious governor promptly complied with the request.

On May 31st, he issued a proclamation to all the magistrates of the colony designating June 4th a general day of thanksgiving for the conclusion of the peace with the Indians and the return of the captives. The magistrates were directed to deliver the same "to the reverend ministers of God's word, that it may be by them communicated from the altar to the community."

CHAPTER VIII.

INTERNAL AFFFAIRS

DURING the war and the negotiations for peace and the return of the captives, little else of interest occurred at Wildwyck. During the fall of 1663 the magistrates of the court on the one side and dominie Blom and the consistory of the church on the other, got into an angry controversy. Each claimed the right to administer upon the estates of persons dying without heirs. Tjerck Claesen de Wit, curator of the estate of William Jansen Seba, was enjoined by the consistory from rendering his account, and Cornelis Barentsen Slecht from paying any of the bills of Seba. The dominie sent a letter to the magistrates telling them that the consistory could not legally release the estate because they came to it ecclesiastically, "not that it was seized by the consistory as the Honorable Court dares falsely to assert."

Then the good dominie raps the court by saying that the consistory "is really astonished that the Honorable Court meets on Sunday, as there are enough other days in the week, and this is the reason why the Magistrates pew in the church is vacant Sunday morning and afternoon." The court referred the whole matter to Stuyvesant. Stuyvesant wrote the consistory that it was the duty of the magistrates to appoint administrators and orphanmasters, have estates inventoried and properly administered. The consistory had nothing to do with such matters. If the consistory or overseers of the poor had a claim against an estate they should proceed according to law and get an order of attachment. As to the complaint of the dominie that the magistrates claimed the right to dispose of what was collected in the community for the church or the poor, he tells the consistory and the magistrates that such funds should remain in the hands of the consistory. He admonished both parties "to remain within the bounderies of their respective positions and to continue, as well officially as privately, to live together in mutual friendship and harmony." To this Blom made answer that the consistory had done no more than to send its clerk to Slecht to request him not to give up the surplus of estates before the consistory had examined whether the overseers of the poor were authorized to receive it. That they maintained that position. They had no desire to meddle in matters belonging to the civil authorities, as they had enough to do in attending to their own duties.

Schout Swartwout and Magistrates Gybertsen, deWit, Chambers and van Imbroch then undertook to lecture Stuyvesant. They wrote him that they were "highly astonished" that he had taken away the small privileges of the village and destroyed their authority by directing that the surplus of estates should be placed in the hands of the overseers of the poor. If such order was to stand they asked that he would: "transfer not only part, but all the duties and rights of the commissioners to Dominie Blom and his consistory, Albert Heymansen, for before or during our time no deacon has been elected who could either read or write, except the Dominie alone, who sides with Albert Heymansen, who has shown himself more than once as an instigator of quarrels."

This letter aroused the ire of the governor. He immediately, December 19, 1663, suspended Schout Swartwout from office and appointed Mathys Capito as clerk. He characterized their letter as insolent. He told the magistrates that if they resigned their office they must remove from the village and its jurisdiction within six months. Captain Cregier, who was the bearer of the governor's letter, was authorized "to fill the places of the obstinate and evil-minded officers by others, selected from the most pious and honest inhabitants."

The magistrates did not resign. Swartwout stood it being out of office until February 14, 1664, when he petitioned Stuyvesant and his council to reinstate him. He says that he had been induced to sign the letter "by fair words, persuasions and impositions." He had made a grave mistake which he regrets "from the bottom of his heart." He had always acted honestly and piously. He was "burdened with a wife and eight small children" and needed the emoluments of the office for the support of his family. He "humbly prays and requests" that he be pardoned. He promises to serve as Schout "honestly and faithfully, with due regard and obedience to his superiors, and courtesy, urbanity, modesty, temperateness and simplicity toward the inhabitants." He was reinstated by order dated February 14, 1664, which order states that he is graciously forgiven this time in hope of amendment, although his unfitness to act as Schout has several times been apparent.

In January, 1664, Ensign Niessen wrote Stuyvesant that a "strange disease afflicted the people but the Almighty's will be done."

In April, 1664, Chambers and van Imbroch petition that the jurisdiction of the court be enlarged to the same extent as the court at Fort Orange. That as cases often came up which required a prompt remedy and as during the winter season no news could be obtained from Manhattan that the court be authorized to enact and enforce provisional ordinances for the good and welfare of the village. That instructions be given to the court messenger as to his duties. Whether the Schout or the Secretary should act as auctioneer. Whether the duties of jailer and executioner belonged to the Schout or the Secretary. That as the school master was "making rather absurd demands for school money from the children, which compels many people to keep their children at home," a fair salary be granted him. That the tapsters' impost on beer, wine, brandy, and distilled waters be let annually by the court and that the same be applied to the expense of the village. That no one be allowed to sell drinks before he has obtained a tapsters' license. The request that the court be allowed to enact ordinances was granted provided that the same, with the reasons for their necessity, be first submitted to the governor and council and their approval obtained. If this could not be done during the winter season or other inconvience the court might execute provisional orders in an emergency on condition that they be submitted for confirmation at the first opportunity. Before anything was done toward giving the schoolmaster a salary the council desired to be informed how much the people paid him. An order defining the duties of the clerk was issued. Sales at voluntary auctions were to be conducted by the clerk or secretary. All Schouts and involuntary sales by the Schout. The tapsters' excise should be let publicly to the highest bidder. One-half the proceeds should be used to pay the debts of the village. No one should sell beer or liquors without permission.

To encourage the people to rebuild the New Village, Stuyvesant arranged to erect there a "stockaded place of refuge and keep there provisionally one-half of the garrison at Wildwyck." For this purpose he ordered hemlock planks to be sent from Fort Orange.

In July, 1664, Stuyvesant and his council, deeming it necessary to have a representative at Wildwyck, who should have general charge of all matters, appointed Wilhelm Beeckman commissary. Every person at Wildwyck was directed to obey his orders. He was to make an inventory of all property belonging to the company and receive the balance there might be in the hands of Ensign Niessen, Matthys Capito, the clerk, and Jacob Burhans, the collector. All goods sent for the garrison were to be consigned and charged to him. He was to convene the Schepens, preside at the meetings of the court and in case of a tie have the casting vote. Whenever he was a party to a suit or acted for the Lords Patroons or on behalf of the law for the Hon. Fiscall, he must leave the bench and have no vote. In his place one of the Schepens should preside. In the absence of the governor or his deputy he had supreme command. He must uphold the law to the best of his knowledge in both civil and military matters. He was to take care that the provisions of the late treaty with the Indians were enforced. He should, at the first opportunity, let out the tapsters' excise.

Beeckman first sat as presiding officer of the court on July 14, 1664. Our old friend Swartwout had at last forever lost his office.

The affairs of New Netherland were in bad shape. The Indian war had been expensive. The treasury was empty. Discontent existed everywhere. The English towns on Long Island had revolted and set up a government of their own. In March, 1664, Stuyvesant turned to the people. At the request of the Burgomasters and Schepens of New Amsterdam he and his council convoked a general assembly of delegates from the several towns to take into consideration the state of the province. This was the first the principle of popular representation was fully recognized in the colony. Wildwyck chose Thomas Chambers and Gysbert van Imborch as delegates. The record of this, the first election in Ulster County and the first direct participation of the people in the management of the government, runs as follows:

"Election held March 31, 1664, by a plurality of votes, for the purpose of sending two delegates from the village of Wildwyck to the Manhattans to a formal Assembly. Whereas, according to a written invitation of the Director-General and Council of New Netherland to the Schout and Commissaries here, dated March 18th last, it was requested that two delegates from our village of Wildwyck be sent to a formal gathering of an Assembly, the Schout and Commissaries have, therefore, called upon us, the undersigned inhabitants of Wildwyck, to meet together on the day named below to select two able persons of the community, and to depute them as delegates to the said meeting, which is to take place on April 10. We have, therefore, selected, by a plurality of votes, the worthy persons, Thomas Chambers and Gysbert van Imborch, to whom we hereby give full power and authority to do what may be necessary for the common interest and that of this place, and also to act in any matter as shall seem to them advisable, confirming what they, the delegates may, according to their obligation, have lawfully done for the common welfare. For which purpose we have personally subscribed to these presents, at Wildwyck, this March 31, 1664. Albert Gysbertsen, Tjerck Claesen deWitt, Cornelis Berentsen Slecht, Evert Pels, Albert Gysbertsen, Juriaen Westphael, Jan Willemse Hoochteylingh, Aert Jacobs, Ariaen Gerretsen van Vliet, Aert Martensen Doorn, Pieter Jacobsen, Mattys Roelofson, Jan Broersen, Jacob Barents Cool Henderick Jochemsen." Of the above all but deWitt, Slecht, Pels, Jacobs and Jochemsen sign by their mark.

The convention met in the city hall at New Amsterdam April 10, 1664. Delegates were present from the towns of New Amsterdam, Rensselaersyck, Fort Orange, Wildwyck, New Haerlem, Staten Island, Breukelen, Midwout, Amersfoort, New Utrecht, Boswyck and Bergen. Its proceedings need not concern us here as they had no bearing on the affairs of Wildwyck.

In accordance with Dutch custom the excise was "farmed out." That is the right to collect and receive the tax imposed on those using liquors was sold at auction to the highest bidder, who was called the "farmer of the excise." The lowest bid that would be received was stated by the auctioneer, who began with a high price and gradually reduced the same until a bid was received. The profit of the farmer was the difference between the amount he received for taxes and the sum bid by him.

July 22, 1664, the court fixed the excise as follows: For an anker (about 10 gallons) of brandy, Spanish wine, distilled waters or others of the same quality, thirty stivers. For an anker of French wine, Rhine wine, wormwood wine or others of the same quality, fifteen stivers, a hogshead to be reckoned as five ankers. For a tun of good beer, one guilder. For a tun of small beer, six stivers. Larger or smaller casks in proportion. The excise must be paid to the farmer in good braided sewan, twelve white or six black beads for one stiver. The farmer must pay one-quarter of the sum bid by him every three months in the same currency at the same rates. The auction was held on the same day with the following result, the sums bid being expressed in florins (a florin forty cents): Tjerck Claesen (de Witt) bids 50; Tomas Harmens, 75; Tjerck Claesen, 100; Tomas Harmans, 125; Evert Pels, 150; Roelof Swartwout, 175; Evert Pels, 200; Tomas Harmens, 225; Tomas Harmensen, 250; Roelof Swartwout, 275; Tomas Harmensen, 300; Tomas Harmensen, 325, Tomas Harmensen, 350. Tomas Harmensen was the successful bidder and gave Tjerck Claesen de Wit and Waldran du Mont as sureties for the faithful performance of his duties.

On August 16, 1664, the court ordered that no "innkeeper or vendor of wine or beer" should sell without first obtaining a license from the court, which must be renewed every three months, and for which he must pay every time "for the use of the judges," one pound Flemish under penalty of suspension of his business. Those who made a business of brewing and distilling brandy must not tap or sell wine by measure.

This was the last judicial and legislative act of the court under Dutch domination. New Netherland surrendered to the English September 6, 1664. On September 1, 1664, the court directed the "burghery and inhabitants" to keep watch for the coming of the English. On the 4th, replying to the question of the Schout as to what should be done in case the English approached the village, it was directed that: "at the discharge of a cannon, all the burghery shall repair to the head watch, there to receive further orders, and that in the meantime the Honorable Schout, together with the Honorable Court, shall seek to parley with said English beyond the gates. Meanwhile the burgher officers are recommended to ascertain what powder and shot there are among the burghery, as we cannot tell how the savages will act in these circumstances."

CHAPTER IX
THE COMING OF THE ENGLISH

THIS is not the place to discuss the justice of the claim of England to New Netherland. On the 12th of March, 1664, King Charles II, by royal patent granted to James, Duke of York, afterward James II, all of New Netherland, to be held by him in free and common socage under the yearly rent of forty beaver skins when demanded. The duke lost no time in taking possession of his domain. Several men-at-war, carrying about four hundred and fifty of the king's soldiers, were dispatched to New Netherland. Richard Nicolls was appointed commander-in-chief of the forces and governor of New Netherland. The fleet arrived at New Amsterdam in August. Resistance was useless. The fort contained but few soldiers. Ammunition was short. The guns of the fleet were trained upon the town. Stuyvesant held out to the last but finally, upon the almost unanimous prayer of the people, frantic at the thought of war and the destruction of their homes, consented to surrender.

Articles of capitulation were signed by Nicolls on September 6th, and ratified by Stuyvesant and his council on the 8th. The Dutch troops, headed by Stuyvesant, with "arms fixed, colors flying, drum beating and matches lighted," marched out of Fort Amsterdam and embarked for Holland. An English guard took possession of the fort. The ensign of the United Provinces was lowered and the flag of England flung to the breeze.

The articles of capitulation provided that all people should continue free denizens and enjoy their lands, houses and goods and dispose of them as they pleased. Those desiring to remove from the country were given a year and six weeks in which to do so. The Dutch should continue to enjoy the liberty of conscience in divine worship and church discipline, and have their own customs concerning inheritances. No judgment that had been given by any court should be questioned. All contracts and bargains made before the surrender should be determined according to the manner of the Dutch. All inferior civil officers and magistrates should, if they pleased, continue until the customary time of election and then new ones to be chosen by themselves.

In September, Nicolls sent Colonel George Cartwright with a detachment of troops to take possession of Fort Orange and Wildwyck. The name of the former was changed to Albany after the Scotch title of the Duke. On his return from Albany, in the latter part of September, 1664, Cartwright stopped off at Wildwyck. No opposition was shown. The local officers were retained in power. A company of soldiers were left in the fort under the command of Daniel Brodhead, an officer in the English army who had come over with Nicolls. In 1669, Governor Lovelace, who had succeeded Nicolls, appointed a commission to regulate and settle the affairs of Esopus and the adjacent villages. On September 17, the commission named the New Village, which had been rebuilt after its destruction by the Indians in 1663, "Hurley," after the ancestral seat of Governor Lovelace's family in Berkshire, England.

A little settlement had grown up southwest of the New Village which, on the same day, was named "Marbletown," probably from the character of the rocks abounding there.

On September 25th, the commission changed the name of Wildwyck to "Kingston," also in honor of the governor, the family seat of whose mother was at Kingston Lisle, Berkshire.

Nine years under Dutch rule passed away. Kingston and the adjacent villages had grown in numbers and importance. In July, 1672, war broke out between the Netherlands and England and France. August 7, 1673, a Dutch fleet under the command of Admirals Cornelis Evertsen and Jacob Benckes sailed up the harbor of New York and trained its guns on the city which, on August 9th, surrendered. Evertsen and Benckes, together with Anthony Colve, Nicoles Boes and Abram Ferdinandus van Zyll, captains in the fleet, constituted themselves a council of war and assumed the reins of government. Colve was selected as Governor General. A proclamation was issued seizing all the property and debts belonging to the kings of France and England or their subjects. Two hundred troops were sent to reduce Albany and Kingston. News of the surrender soon reached Kingston. On August 5th, 1673, the magistrates directed Everdt Pels and Robert Gouldsberry to go to New York and ascertain the condition of affairs: "because we have been informed that there are some Holland vessels there for the purpose of taking the country." Each was to receive a schepel of wheat per day for his trouble. It was further ordered that a man should keep watch at the Ronduyt and that Captain Chambers, at the last report, should call the burghers to arms and then send some delegates to the troops. In the meantime to act in accordance with the report of the messengers.

The following proclamation was issued: "We, the magistrates, burghers and residents of the village of Kingston and jurisdiction of the same, declare under oath that owing to the surrender of the country, hitherto called New York, on account of which we have been discharged from the oath of allegiance taken to his majesty of Great Britain, we absolutely submit to the authority of their High Mightinesses the Lords States General of the United Netherlands and his serene highness the prince of Orange, to be true and faithful to them and at the least written notice of him who shall be here in authority, or should be authorized by him for said purpose, to keep ourselves in readiness against all enemies whoever they may be, for the purpose of assisting to protect the rights of their High Mightinesses as it is the duty of all pious and faithful subjects. But, whereas, there are several people living here who are native-born Englishmen, therefore, they are permitted, in case it should happen that we should be inimically attacked here by the order of his royal majesty of Great Britain to remain quiet and to remain unarmed without in any manner taking part in it. But in case with the aforesaid English any enemies of whatever other nation should be allied then the English residents here shall be obliged to defend themselves against them by every possible means without being permitted to take the least exception."

August 26th, the magistrates requested some of the oldest burghers to give their views in writing "within twice twenty-four hours" as to what matters concerning the village should be made to the "vigorous council of war" at New York, and Joost Adriaensen and the secretary, W. Montagne, were dispatched to New York for that purpose. These representatives appeared before the council of war which, on September 1, 1673, changed the name of Kingston to "Swaenenburgh," after the flag ship of Admiral Evertsen. The council directed that the towns of Swaenenburgh, Horley, and Marbletowne should "conjointly nominate by their deputies" three persons for Schout and three for secretary, from which the council would select a Schout and Secretary for the three towns. The "commonalty" of Swaenenburgh should nominate eight persons as schepens. Hurley and Marbletowne having been under one bench of justice should continue so, and they should nominate eight persons as schepens. From the persons so nominated the council would select the magistrates. A double number should in like manner be nominated for chief officers of the militia. No one unless of the Reformed religion must be nominated and none unless they were at least friendly to the Dutch.

From the nominees so made the council, on October 6, 1673, named the following officers:

For magistrates of Swaenenburg, Cornelis Wyncoop, Roeloff Kierstede, Wessell Ten Broeck, Jan Burhans.

For officers of the militia, Captain Mathys Mathysen, Lieutenant Jan Willemsen, Ensign Mathys Barentsen.

For magistrates of Hurley and Marble town, Louis DuBois, Roeloff Hendricksen, Jan Joosten, Jan Broersen.

For officers of the militia, Captain Albert Heymans, Lieutenant Jan Broersen, Ensign Gerrit Adriaensen.

For secretary of the three towns, William Lamontagne.

William Beeckman, who had been nominated for Schout, had removed to New York and declined. The inhabitants were directed to nominate another person by "plurality of votes," and Isaac Grevenraet was nominated and appointed. An order defining the duties and powers of the schout and magistrates was issued. It substantially restored the government to the form it had been under Stuyvesant.

The council of war made but few orders relating to the three villages. The inhabitants of Hurley were commanded "not to remove their dwellings outside the village" unless they obtain special consent. The schout was refused a salary because none had ever been allowed. He was to act as auctioneer and with the secretary collect the excise. The Burgher Watch was to assist him "in arresting evildoers." The magistrates must see to it that good watch be kept "to which end some of the burghers should repair every evening, about sunset, to the usual guard house, and not leave before sunrise." They should see that the officers of the militia were respected and obeyed by their men. Their arms must be inspected and they must be supplied with ammunition. During this brief period of Dutch rule little of interest happened in the villages. The courts found little to do. The stockade was ordered repaired. Roelof Kierstede and Alberdt Jansen were appointed fire wardens and directed to inspect all chimneys every two weeks and see that they were kept clean. Every person must clean the street in front of his house of refuse and dirt.

Hendrick van Wyen was fined one hundred guilders for assaulting Gretje Westercam and, in addition, was condemned to pay the fees and expenses of the doctor. One-fourth of the fine went to the poor, one-fourth for the village and one-half to the officers. Anna Nottingham was. fined one hundred guilders for calling Schout Grevenraet a "hungry cur" and a "hungry raven." Klaes Tysen sued Cornelis Wynkoop for four hundred schepels of wheat, the price of a negro sold him. Wynkoop defended on the ground that the negro was represented to be "hale and sound" whereas he had lost a finger and another finger and a thumb were stiff. The court referred the matter to arbitrators who reported that the negro was not sound and Tysen must take him back. The decision was approved by the court. Robberdt Biggerstab brought an action against Jan Gerretsen for damage for running over his pig. "Defendant says that when he was passing with his wagon he heard a pig squeal. His wife, going to the spot, found no pig." Plaintiff was ordered to prove his case. What became of the litigation or of the pig the record does not disclose. Dutch supremacy continued but for a brief period. A treaty of peace between England and the Netherlands was signed at Westminster February 19, 1674. By it New York was restored to the English. The King commissioned Edmund Andros governor of New York, July 1, 1674.

TREATY WITH THE INDIANS.

On July 7, 1674, the State's General dispatched an order to Governor Colve to deliver New Netherland to Andros. The order reached Colve October 15, 1674, and on November 10, 1674, the formal surrender took place at New York. Andros appointed George Hall sheriff and Robert Peacock constable of Kingston. Cornelis Wyncoop, J. Adriaensen and George Hall, who had been magistrates at Kingston on its surrender to the Dutch, were reinstated in office. December 20, 1674, the old court met for the last time.

Schout Grevenraet presented an order of Governor Andros relieving the magistrates from the oath of allegiance they had taken to the State's General and the Prince of Orange. The order reinstating the old magistrates was published. They immediately took the oath of allegiance to King James.

The new court convened January 12, 1675. The sceptre swayed by the Dutch over New Netherland, from the day that Henry Hudson sailed up the river that bears his name, forever ceased to govern.

CHAPTER X.

GOVERNMENT

FOR a correct understanding of the character of the government under which the people of Wildwyck lived a brief sketch of the legislative and judicial history of New Netherland should be given. June 3, 1661, the State's General of the United Provinces granted a charter of incorporation to the West India Company. It was an era of commercial monopoly and the charter was characteristic of the age. Not only was the company given a monopoly of trade in all the Dutch possessions in America, but it was invested with full powers of government. The will of the company, as expressed in its orders, was to be the law of New Netherland. The general supervision and management of the company was lodged in a board or chamber of nineteen members, distributed among different cities of Holland. The affairs of New Netherland were committed to the chamber of Amsterdam. In 1624 the company appointed Peter Minuit Director General of New Netherland and a council of five members to assist him. To them was given supreme authority in the colony. They were also the tribunal for the trial of all cases, civil and criminal. To encourage emigration the West India Company, in 1629, granted the famous charter of "Freedoms and Exemptions." Under its provisions any member of the company who should, within four years, plant a colony of fifty persons, upwards of fifteen years of age, in any part of New Netherland, except the island of Manhattan, which the company reserved to itself, would be acknowledged a "Patroon of New Netherland." His colony could extend sixteen miles along the one side of the river or eight miles on each side and as far into the country as the situation would permit.

He became sole owner of the territory with the right to dispose of it by will. He was chief magistrate of his estate. He could create courts from which, if the matter in dispute involved more than fifty guilders, an appeal could be taken to the Director-General and Council. Kiliaen van Rensselaer, one of the directors of the company, in 1629 and 1630 purchased large tracks of land from the Indians lying on both sides of the river near Albany. Under the charter he became the feudal lord of a vast estate embracing most of the present counties of Rensselaer, Columbia, and Albany, except Fort Orange and the land immediately about it. This immense estate was named the manor or colony of Rensselaerswyck. Most of the early settlers at Wildwyck came from it. The settlers at Rensselaerswyck were the mere tenants of the Patroon. Within his domain he claimed and exercised exclusive jurisdiction.

No appeal was allowed to the Director General and Council at Manhattan. On the other hand the governor and council claimed that the manor was subject to their jurisdiction. This led to an angry controversy between the parties lasting during all the history of the colony. At the request of Governor Kieft, in 1641, the masters and heads of families, residents of New Amsterdam, elected "Twelve Select Men" to consider public matters. This was the first the people had been recognized. Kieft and his council paid but little attention to their proceedings and soon forbade them to hold any further meetings, "as they tend to dangerous consequences, and to the serious injury both of the country and our authority." In 1643 the impending war with the Indians compelled Kieft to again turn to the people. A board of "Eight Men" were chosen to consider affairs. Beyond sending a memorial to the company and the States General describing the deplorable condition of the colony they did but little. July 7, 1645, the West India Company adopted an ordinance providing that thereafter the Supreme Council in New Netherland should consist of the Director General, a Vice Director and a Schout Fiscall. Provided, that in all cases in which the Schout Fiscall acted for the company, the military commander should sit in his stead, and, were the charge criminal, two persons should be "adjoined from the commonalty of that district where the crime was perpetrated." The company appointed Petrus Stuyvesant, Director; Lubbertus Van Binclage, Vice-Director, and Hendrick Van Dyck, Schout Fiscall. In 1647 Stuyvesant found the treasury empty; the fort in need of repairs; the Indians threatening. It was thought wise to give the people some small voice in the government. So in August, 1647, an order was issued to the people to elect eighteen of the most "expert and reasonable persons" from whom the Director-General and Council would select "Nine Men as is customary in Fatherland," to give their advice when called on and to assist in promoting the welfare of the country. Eighteen persons were elected from whom the Director-General and Council chose the "Nine Men." They were directed not to assist at private conventicles or meetings without the knowledge and advice of the Director and Council. Three of their number should once a week be admitted to the council, as long as civil cases were before it, and act as arbitrators in matters referred to them. The term of six expired annually. Twelve to succeed them should be nominated by the sitting board and from the twelve and the sitting board six should be chosen. The "Nine Men" represented Manhattan, Breukelen, Amersfoort, and Pavonia. They acted only in an advisory capacity. In 1650 the States General recommended to the company that New Amsterdam be granted a burgher government. With great reluctance the company, in 1652, directed that a municipal government be established to consist of one Schout, two Burgomasters, and five Schepens, to be elected by the citizens in the manner usual in "this city of Amsterdam," to act as a court of justice with the right of appeal in certain cases to the Supreme Court of Judicature. In order to understand the nature of the government to be established for New Amsterdam we must turn to the political institutions of old Amsterdam. Burgher right was a very old institution in Holland. From a very early period, "the exclusive right to trade in Amsterdam was confined by law to such of its inhabitants as were burghers either by birth, purchase, intermarriage, or by a vote of the city." Native citizens acquired the right on becoming of age and registering their names; the others after the lapse of a year from the time of their enrollment. Burgher right conferred upon the holder not only freedom of trade but opened to him all offices under the city government. "He could not be arrested or imprisoned if he could procure bail, nor indicted nor tried for an offense after the term of one year." "If found guilty of a capital charge he was saved from attaint of blood and confiscation of property." Women could become burghers but, if the right was obtained by purchase, it could only be enjoyed while they were unmarried or widows. They lost it if married to those not burghers and their children did not inherit the parent's privilege. On the death of the husband the mother was reinstated in her privileges. In 1652 the burghers of Amsterdam were divided into two classes, "Great and Small, giving to the wealthy for the sum of five hundred guilders ($200) the privilege of enrolling their names on the list of 'The Great' who, alone, were to be invested with the monopoly of all offices and the exemption from confiscation and attainder in case of conviction of capital offences." The "Small" burghers had only freedom of trade and the privilege of being received into the different guilds. By an ordinance adopted in 1657 the "Great" and "Small" burgher right was introduced in New Netherland.

The "Great Burgher Right" was granted:—

First. To those who had been or were in the high or supreme government of the country and their descendants in the male line.

Second. To all former and actual Burgomasters and Schepens of New Amsterdam and their descendants in the male line.

Third. To all former ministers of the gospel and those then in office and their descendants in the male line.

Fourth. To the commissioned officers of the militia, including the ensign, and their descendants in the male line, provided that they or their descendants in the male line had not lost or forfeited burgher right by not keeping "fire and light" agreeable to the custom of the city of Amsterdam.

Fifth. To all others on payment of the sum of fifty guilders.

The "Small Burgher Right" was given:—

First. To all those who had resided and kept fire and light within the city for one year and six weeks.

Second. To all born within the city.

Third. To all who had or should marry native born daughters of burghers, provided the burgher right had not been lost or forfeited by absence from the city or by not keeping fire and light within the city for one year and six weeks.

All persons who now or hereafter keep any shop, "however it may be called," in the city or its jurisdiction were bound to apply to the Burgomasters for the "Small Right" and pay twenty guilders for the same.

All servants of the company under wages, all passengers and new comers who settled elsewhere, provided they did so within six weeks were exempt from applying for the right for the exercise of "all sorts of handicraft and the practice thereof." It was refused to the Jews.

When this ordinance was first proclaimed only twenty persons applied for the "Great Right." Among them was Rachel Van Tienhoven, the widow or deserted wife of Cornelis Van Tienhoven. By an ordinance adopted in 1660 it was provided:—"That no newly arrived traders, Scotch factors or merchants shall be at liberty to transport or to send their goods from here to Fort Orange, or elsewhere, within the district of New Netherland, unless they have previously obtained burgher right here."

The government of the city of Amsterdam consisted of one Schout, four Burgomasters, nine Schepens, and a council of thirty-six members. The Schout, Burgomasters and Schepens composed a board called "the Lords of the Court of the city of Amsterdam." They were vested with the right to make all city laws and ordinances and had jurisdiction of all civil and criminal cases. The office of Schout was one of the most important both in Amsterdam and New Netherland. His powers and duties combined those of our sheriff and district attorney. He convened the court, presided at its meetings, proposed matters for consideration, counted and declared the votes. He prosecuted all offenders against the law and did not in such matters sit as a member of the court. Unless an offense was committed in his presence he could not arrest any person without first taking an information before the court in regard to the crime. He executed all judgments of the court. In Amsterdam on the first of each year, all who had served as Burgomasters or as Schepens chose three persons to succeed those retiring. The three chose one other person and these constituted the Board of Burgomasters. They were the chief rulers of the city, "the principal church wardens; the guardians of the poor, of widows and orphans; and without their consent, no woman or minor could execute any legal instrument." Each Burgomaster attended daily, in rotation, during three months of the year, in the city hall, for the dispatch of public business, thus resembling our mayor. In January of each year the city council nominated fourteen citizens as Schepens to the Stadtholder, from whom nine were chosen as Schepens. They entered upon their duties February second or Candlemas day. They constituted a court of almost unlimited civil and criminal jurisdiction. The Burgomasters and Schepens, when assembled together, exercised legislative powers for municipal purposes.

Although the order of the West India Company directed that the Schout, Burgomasters and Schepens, who should constitute the government and court for New Amsterdam should be elected, Stuyvesant, who understood the real wishes of his employers, appointed all of them. This court was known as the court of the Schout, Burgomasters and Schepens. It had jurisdiction of all cases except capital. It also acted as a board of aldermen in municipal matters.

The Director General and Council reserved the right "to make ordinances or publish particular interdicts even for New Amsterdam. This court was created for and had jurisdiction only in New Amsterdam which, at the time, was understood to embrace only the lower part of the island of Manhattan. Similar courts, varied in their powers and duties as circumstances required, were established by orders of the council at Fort Orange, in the settlements on Long Island and at Wildwyck. Their jurisdiction and duties were prescribed in the ordinances creating them.

Such was the government of New Netherland. Government by the people, through their representatives, did not exist. The grand jury and trial by jury was unknown. The law of the land was to be found in the ancient customs and laws of the city of Amsterdam, and the ordinances enacted by the Director-General and Council.

These ordinances embraced a wide range of subjects and touched the daily life of the citizen at almost every point. Banns of marriage must be published or proclaimed in the place where the parties resided. Stuyvesant would not allow the flimsy excuses or squeamishness of prospective bridgegroom or bride to interfere with the rapid populating of the colony; neither would he stand for anything save the martial relation. So, it was enacted that after the third proclamation of banns the parties should, "if no lawful impediment occurs, cause their marriages to be solemnized within one month at the furthest, after the last proclamation, or within that time, appear and show cause where they ought, for refusing; and that on pain of forfeiting ten guilders for the first week of the aforesaid month, and for the succeeding weeks twenty guilders for each week, until they have made known the reasons for refusing." Dominie Blom notified his congregation at Wildwyck that he would enforce this ordinance. No man and woman should be at liberty, "to keep house as married persons before and until they are lawfully married, on pain of forfeiting one hundred guilders, more or less, as their quality shall be found to warrant, and all such persons may be amerced every month by the officer, according to the order and custom of our Fatherland."

None but legal weights and measures could be used and those were the ones in use in the city of Amsterdam.

To prevent damage to growing crops by animals running at large three persons should be appointed fence viewers for each village. They must inspect all fences and see that all persons who did not keep them tight were fined. A pound must be established in each village in which any person could impound all cattle found in the corn fields. Before they could be released the owner must pay six florins for a horse, four for an ox or cow, two for a calf, hog or sheep; one-half of which went to the pound keeper, the other half to the impounder or whoever made the complaint. If the animals were not released by sunset the fines were doubled and if not released on the second day, they were sold at public auction to the highest bidder.

Smuggling was strictly prohibited. Ordinance after ordinance prohibiting the sale of intoxicating liquors to the Indians was passed. Although every one recognized that this traffic was at the bottom of most of the troubles with the red men it could not be stopped. Slavery existed in New Netherland at a very early period and the settlers at Wildwyck held the black man in bondage. The support of the poor was, to some extent, left to the church. The magistrates appointed two persons "who shall go around every Sunday with a little bag among the congregation and collect the alms for the support of the poor of that place." In addition a part of the fines imposed by the courts for the violation of ordinances went for their maintenance.

All fighting, wounding, drawing of knives and assaults were forbidden under heavy penalties.

The observance of Sunday was strictly enjoined. No beer or liquor could be sold. No ordinary labor performed. No sports or games allowed. In order to prevent the waste of powder, carousing and accidents, all firing of guns, beating of drums, planting of May poles and the retailing of beer or liquor on New Year or May days was prohibited. No liquor or beer could be sold without license and payment of the excise. No tavern keeper could brew beer or liquor and no brewer sell at retail. In 1658 the maximum price that could be charged by brewers was fixed at, for a ton (about 40 gallons) of strong beer, ten guilders in silver, 15 in beaver, 22 in wampum. A ton of small beer, 3 guilders in silver, 4 and one-half in beaver, 6 in wampum. By tavern keepers one-half gallon of beer, 6 stivers in silver, 9 in beaver, 12 in wampum. A can of French wine, 18 stivers in silver, 22 in beaver, 36 in wampum. A can of Spanish wine, 24 stivers in silver, 36 in beaver, 50 in wampum. A gill of brandy, 5 stivers in silver, 7 in beaver, 10 in wampum.

In the same year the price of bread was fixed at a coarse wheat loaf, eight pounds, 7 stivers in silver, 10 in beaver, 14 in wampum. A rye loaf, eight pounds, 6 stivers in silver, 9 in beaver, 12 in wampum. A white loaf, two pounds, 4 stivers in silver, 6 in beaver, 8 in wampum.

Little, if any, coin circulated in the colony. The zeawan or wampum of the Indians was the circulating medium. Wheat and other grain was also used as a medium of exchange. Fines and penalties were imposed and debts paid in either. Wampum was made by the Indians from the inner surface of the shell of the clam and periwinkle. They were worked out into beads, mostly of two colors, white and a very dark purple, or black. They were generally cylindrical, being about ⅛ to 7/16 in. in length and about ⅛ to 3/16 in. in diameter. They were strung upon cords, these fastened together made a belt. Wampum was highly prized by the Indians. Necklaces of the same were used for personal adornment. Belts as a badge of rank and official dignity and in the ratification of treaties and solemn agreements. Many ordinances were passed regulating the use and value of wampum as currency. In 1641 six strung beads passed for one stiver. In 1650 six white and three black strung for a stiver. In 1658 eight white and four black for a stiver. In 1663 eight white or four black for a stiver. During the same year the price of a beaver in silver was eight guilders and a muddle and a half of wheat was worth one beaver, or about thirty cents a bushel.

The revenue for the colony was derived from an export duty on furs, duties on imported goods and the tenths of argricultural products reserved by the government as a consideration for lands granted. The revenue for the villages was obtained from an excise tax on liquors and beer, a tax on slaughtered cattle, and all or a part of the fines imposed on individuals for the violation of ordinances. A land tax was also imposed for various purposes.

As early as 1659 the people of Wildwyck had asked that a court be established so that everybody "could be made to go along." Their request was not complied with until May 16, 1661, on which day the Director-General and Council adopted an ordinance creating a court for Wildwyck. Evert Pels, Cornelis Barentsen Sleght and Elbert Heymans Rose (Roosa) were appointed Schepens for the term of one year from the last of May, 1661. After the first year there were four Schepens. Before the expiration of each year the court transmitted to the council a list of "honest and decent persons," from whom two were appointed in the place of two retiring. Two remained in office "in order to inform the new," thus two served for two years. The Schepens must be "honest, intelligent persons, owners of real estate, promoters and professors of the Reformed religion."

During the existence of the court the Schepens were:—May, 1661, to May, 1662, Evert Pels, Cornelis Barentsen Sleght, Elbert Heymans Rose. May, 1662, to May, 1663, Pels, Rose, Albert Gysbertsen, Tjirick deWit. May, 1663, to May, 1664, Gysbertsen, deWit, Thomas Chambers, Gysbert van Imbrogh. 1664, Chambers, van Imbrogh, Henderick Jochemsen, Jan Willemsen Hoochteylingh. The West India Company, on April 15,

1660, appointed Roeloff Swartwout Schout of the court, proposed to be established for Wildwyck. As we have seen he had rather a hard time in getting his job. Stuyvesant did not think him fit for the place and only commissioned him upon the pre-emptory order of the company. He was to hold office for four years. He took rank of the Schepens and was president of the court. He published and executed all orders relating to the village. He should see that no "whorehouses, whoremongers, or other similar bad houses" were permitted. He acted as prosecutor in all criminal matters. He made all arrests, examined the prisoner within four days, and within the same time, thereafter, must bring him to trial. He collected the votes of the court and acted as its secretary until one was appointed. If he were a party and when he acted as prosecutor or for the company he had no vote, but must leave the bench and one of the senior Schepens must preside. He received as compensation for his services one-half of all civil fines, one-half of all fees for tax and court notices and one-third of what fell to the village in criminal matters. The court met once a fortnight, "harvest time excepted."

Extraordinary meetings should not be held except upon the request of both parties to a cause who must deposit the costs of the court, three guilders for the president and fifty stivers for each Schepen. The court messenger gave twenty-four hours' notice to the Schepens of the time of holding each session. If any failed to appear, unless excused by sickness or absence, they were fined twenty stivers each and the president forty. Those late in arriving were fined twenty stivers for the benefit of those on time. A Schepen could not sit if he were a party to a suit or related to a party by consanquinity, "such as brothers, brothers-in-law or cousins in the first or direct line." In case of disagreement the minority must coincide with the majority, but could have their opinions entered on the record which must not be made public. The clerk kept the minutes of the proceedings, copies of which were transmitted to the council. He was allowed sixteen stivers for drawing a petition in civil proceedings, twenty in a suit for injuries and criminal cases "of the middle degree," and for a certificate and a copy twenty-four stivers. All judgments rendered by the court were subject to reversal by the Director-General and Council and to them all appeals were taken. The court was given jurisdiction of "all matters touching civil affairs" and could give judgment to the amount of fifty guilders without appeal. If the sum involved was greater the aggrieved party could appeal within ten days after judgment on giving security for the principal and costs of the action. All cases of crime must be referred to the Director-General and Council. The court must take information concerning the offense, arrest and detain the party charged, and send him and the information to the council. "Minor offenses, such as brawls, injuries, scolding, striking with fist, threats, simple drawing of a knife or sword without bloodshed" were left to the decision of the court, the condemned party to have the right of appeal. "All cases of major crimes, and delinquents charged with wounding and bloodshedding, whoredom and adultery, public and notorious theft, robberies, smuggling of contraband articles, blaspheming and profaning God's holy name and religion, slandering and caluminating the Supreme Government or its representatives, shall, after information, affidavits and testimony have been taken, be referred to the Director-General and Council of New Netherland." The grand jury was unkown. The party accused had the right to give bail in all cases except murder, treason, arson and rape.

Two modes of trial existed in criminal matters. One an ordinary public trial in which the ordinary rules of evidence prevailed; the other, an examination before two Schouts, upon written questions. The penalties were fines, imprisonment, whipping, the pillory and death. The court was given no power to enact ordinances, rules or regulations even for village affairs. If they thought any such necessary they must be submitted to the council for its approval. In 1664 this provision was so far modified as to allow the court to enact "Provisional Ordinances," provided the same, with the reasons for their necessity, be first submitted to the council and its approval obtained. If this could not be done during the winter season or by reason of other inconvenience the court might execute such ordinances in an emergency on condition that they be submitted for confirmation at the first opportunity.

During the Indian war of 1663 Stuyvesant appointed the Schout, Schepens, the commander and lieutenant of the militia, and the captain of the train band, a council of war to take charge of all matters. Acting together they constituted the court during the war. In 1664 Wilhelm Beeckman was appointed commissary for Wildwyck. He also acted as Schout. He presided at the meetings of the court and in case of a tie had the casting vote. In the absence of the governor or his deputy he had supreme command.

The practice in the court was simple. A summons commanding the party to appear at the next session of the court was served on the defendant at least one day before the meeting. "In case of arrest, or difference between strangers, when it may be served on the very day of the session." If defendant did not appear he could not thereafter question the jurisdiction of the court and was condemned to pay the cost of the summons. A second summons was then served and if defendant still failed to appear he was subject to additional costs. A third summons was then served and upon default judgment was rendered. If defendants presence was necessary a warrant of arrest was issued. Each party stated his case and could be sworn as a witness. If the court required further proof an adjournment was had and the testimony of witnesses taken either before the court or by written depositions made before a notary. Documents in the handwriting of a party were presumed to be genuine. Books of account, itemized and correctly kept, were received in evidence. All affidavits, interrogatories, contracts, testaments, agreements, and other important documents in order to be used as evidence must be written by the secretary "or other authorized person unless by necessity it should be impossible to call on such person." Documentory evidence, dying declarations, and testimony supported by two witnesses was termed full proof. The testimony of one witness, half proof. Hearsay testimony was received as half proof and as corrobative evidence.

Matters in controversy were very frequently referred by the court to arbitrators to hear and decide.

Judgments were rendered payable in wampum, wheat or other grain. A specified time in which to pay was usually given. If not paid an execution was issued to the court messenger who demanded payment by the debtor in twenty-four hours. If not paid the messenger, in the presence of two of the Schepens, seized the personal property of the debtor and made an inventory of the same. The property was kept for six days and after notice had been given at one session of the court it was sold the next court day to the highest bidder. If sufficient personal property to pay the judgment could not be found the real estate of the debtor was sold upon four days' notice. Debts due the debtor could be attached and sold.

According to Dutch custom auction sales were continued during the burning of a candle, as it flickered out the property was struck off to the highest bidder.

The court administered the estates of deceased persons and had control of the property of minors in much the same manner as our Surrogates court, by administrators and guardians appointed by it. Deeds, mortgages and other instruments were acknowledged before the court and recorded in its minutes.

The court at Wildwyck held its first session July 12,

1661. Jacob Joosten was appointed court messenger and "to attend to all kinds of church service and services for the court," at the annual salary of two hundred guilders in wampum. Joosten had trouble in getting his pay. Schout Swartwout complained to the court that Joosten was "of little or no service to him," to which he replied that he had only received one hundred and fourteen guilders on account of his salary. The court admonished him to be more faithful in his duty and he would be paid "as soon as possible." Secretary Capito claimed half his fees and Joosten refused to pay. At last, in December, 1663, Jacob Boerhans, the collector, was directed to pay him fifty guilders in wampum out of the excise money on account. In April, 1664, he again asked for his pay and the court gravely informed him that he could not have it because the treasury was empty.

In October, 1661, the court fixed the price that Pieter Jacobsen could charge for grinding corn at eight stivers a bushel in wampum. As to those who had no wampum he could deduct a tenth part of the corn. Each of the parties to a suit were required to pay thirty-six stivers, to be advanced by the plaintiff, and collected from the defeated party, for rent of the court room. Tjerck Claesen deWit, although a Schepen, in a suit against Corenlis Bartensen Slecht, refused to put up the money, whereupon his colleagues on the bench informed him that his witnesses would not be admitted in the court room.

In February, 1664, the court ordered the collector to pay Aert Martensen Doorn forty-two guilders in wampum for rent of the court room. The litigation brought before the court was pretty much of the same nature as that of today. Actions for debt injury to property and slander were frequent. During the Indian war of 1663 a number of persons were fined for going to the fields to work without a guard of troops. The Sunday laws were strictly enforced and fines imposed for violations of the excise ordinances. The court was quite sensitive as to any criticism of its proceedings. Barent Gerretsen and his wife were placed under arrest for having said that the magistrates did not give them justice and because they "have several times poked fun at the court." Hendrick Jochemse was fined twenty-five guilders and Elsjen Jans and Annetjen Aerts six guilders each, to go the poor, "for having used vile and nasty language before the court."

Aeltje Sybrants, wife of Mattys Roelofsen, was fined one hundred guilders for using vile and indecent language to the Schout on his going to her house with the order of the court notifying all persons not to sell strong drink to the Indians. Two-thirds of the fine went to the Schout and one-third to Dominie Blom for the church. Cornelis Barentsen Slecht was confined in the guard house for refusing to render his account in the matter of the estate of William Jansen Seba.

In reading these old records one is impressed with the wonderful perspicuity of the legal documents and papers. All the acumen and sophistry of the modern lawyer could not twist their language into anything but its obvious meaning to any one of ordinary intelligence. The court was not troubled with the interpretation of obscure statutes or the reconciliation of conflicting authorities. Their decisions are clear cut and direct to the point.

They rendered justice, rough and ready perhaps, but exact justice. Here is the complete record of one case, famous in the annals of Ulster County.

"October 4, 1662, Grietjen Westercamp, plaintiff, vs. Pieter Jacobsen, defendant. Default.

October 17, 1662, Grietjen Hendricks Westercamp, plaintiff, vs. Pieter Jacobsen, defendant. Plaintiff demands of defendant why he denies his child. Defendant answers and says, "I have my doubts about it." Plaintiff says that defendant ruined her, and asks that he restore her honor. Defendant denies that he ruined her, and says "she must prove this to me," and also denies that he promised to marry her. He asks her when she became pregnant, and when she was delivered. Plaintiff says that defendant made her pregnant eight days before Christmas, 1661, and that she was delivered eight days before Kermis, 1662. Plaintiff says that she conceived at the mill, house of Pieter Jacobsen. Defendant requests two weeks' time. The Schout and Commissaries grant the defendant two weeks' time, and order plaintiff to prove at the next session that defendant ruined her.

November 1, 1662. Greitjen Hendricks Westercamp, plaintiff, vs. Pieter Jacobsen, defendant. Plaintiff exhibits to the Schout and Commissaries a certificate and deposition by seven women, who certify and declare that they were present at the birth of Grietje Westercamp's child, and that she swore three times that Pieter Jacobsen was the father of the child. The plaintiff asks for a vindication of her honor. The defendant says plaintiff did not behave as a decent girl should, and produces a certificate of Juriaen Westvael and his wife who declare that Grietjen Westercamp lay under one blanket with Jan van Breeman, with his daughter between them. Defendant, being interrogated, admits having conversed and lain with plaintiff, but did not promise marriage, and, besides gave her no money for it, and asks if a woman can be thirteen months and four days in the family way. The Schout and Commissaries order defendant to bring clearer proof at the court's next session.

January 9, 1663. Pieter Jacobsen, plaintiff, vs. Grietjen Westercamp. Plaintiff, by petition, asks to be released from defendant, so as to be a free man again and earn his living. Defendant requests fourteen days' time. The court again allows defendant fourteen days' time, and if she cannot bring proof, plaintiff shall receive the judgment of the court which, upon request, will meter out justice.

January 22, 1663. Pieter Jacobsen, plaintiff, vs. Grietjen Westercamp, defendant. Default.

February 6, 1663. Pieter Jacobsen, plaintiff, vs. Grietjen Westercamp, defendant. Plaintiff asks by petition that the court grant him justice against defendant. Defendant answers that plaintiff is the father of her child. He denies this, says it is not his child, and offers to affirm upon oath. Which he did before the court, saying, "I am not the father of the child: so truly help me God Almighty." Therefore, the court decides to allow plaintiff to marry any other person he pleases, and it is also thought proper, in view of several certificates previously shown by both parties to the court, that plaintiff shall, for the nonce, pay defendant two hundred guilders, on a former acknowledgement made by him that he did not compensate her for lying with her, and he is therefore bound to pay her for that service."

"Most upright judge." "O, upright judge." "O, learned judge." "A second Daniel, a Daniel."

This sad romance had, however, a happy sequel. The records of baptisms and marriages of the Dutch church at Wildwyck kept by Dominie Blom contain the following:—

"1661, October 1

Parents	Name of child and	Witnesses and
Pieter Jacobsen	date of baptism	sponsors
"miller here"	Pieter	Saertje Staets
Grietjen	1 Oct.	Willemje Jacobs
Hendricks		Pieter
Westercamp		Hillebrantsen

1664

Jan Gerretsen, j. m. (young man) of Heerden and Grietjen Hendricks Westercamp, of Amsterdam in Nieunederlant, both resid. here.

"Dst nec virgo nec vidua." First publication of banns, 9 March; second, 16 March; third, 23 March."

Good for you, Dominie Blom. You reversed the judg-ment of the court. You placed the hand of the church upon the head of the child and named him after him who Grietje declared was the father. Good for you, dominie, but you might have stretched a point and left that Latin off the record.

And Grietje, as the record shows, married the very best fellow in all the world and they lived happily together forever and a day. During the entire period covered by this history Stuyvesant was not only Director-General but as matter of fact he was the council. Its members were subservient to his commands. He ruled the colony. His will was law. He was obstinate, hasty, quick to anger, would not brook opposition and held a poor opinion of the people. Their voice did not weigh with him. They were meant to be governed and he was meant to govern them. "We derive our authority from God and the company, not from a few ignorant subjects," he declared, and he believed it and meant it. He was a devout member and a strong supporter of the Dutch Reformed Church. He would tolerate no other form of worship. He persecuted the Lutherans, the Baptists and the Quakers, and endeavored to drive them from the colony. He was a brave man, not moved by popular clamor or abuse. He knew the people and had their welfare at heart. He was an educated man, the son of a Dutch dominie. He believed in the education of the people and founded a public school. He was a thorough Dutchman. He was deeply interested both personally and officially in the welfare of New Netherland. He loved the fatherland with passionate devotion, and gave to her service the best years of his life. His ashes are mingled with the soil of the world's metropolis, whose foundations he helped to lay.

A government by a commercial monopoly could not last in New Netherland. Sooner or later the West India Company would have been compelled to relinquish the reins of power. Sooner or later the people would have governed themselves. They were the descendants of the men and women who had fought at Harlem and at

Leyden, who had waged a hundred years' war for liberty, who had humbled the pride of Phillip II and forever driven the Spaniard from their country. Sooner or later independence from fatherland would have come and sooner or later, if the English had not come, who knows, the birth of a new republic might have been rung out from the bell in the steeple of the little church at Wildwyck, instead of the one in the belfry in Carpenters' Hall, Philadelphia.

CHAPTER XI.

THE CHURCH

THE tenets of Calvinism as established by the Synod of Dordrecht for the Reformed Protestant Dutch Church was the national religion of Holland and of New Netherland. The oath of office, taken by the magistrates of Wildwyck, contained the provision, "that we will maintain and exercise the Reformed Church service and no other." The public exercises of religion were not allowed to any sects in Holland except the Calvinists. But all others were permitted to exercise their worship in private houses, which were in fact as if public, the places of preaching being spacious and of sufficient size for any assembly. The Prince of Orange, on accepting the office of stadtholder, declared to the world that he would "maintain and promote the Reformed religion and no other," but "that he should not suffer any man to be called to account molested, or injured for his faith and conscience." While for reasons of state he was obliged to issue a proclamation prohibiting the public exercise of the Romish religion, the document declared that it was not intended, "to impose any burden, or make inquisition into any man's conscience." Dutchmen for near a century had waged a war to achieve liberty of conscience. What they had obtained for themselves they were willing to grant to all men. Holland became the refuge of the persecuted of every sect and every creed.   Even the Puritan of New England imbibed from her free air, most of the faith for which he has been canonized.   The Lutheran, the Baptist, the Quaker, the Jew, and the Catholic found a home in New Netherland and a place to worship God according to the dictates of their own conscience.   But now, at the call of religious fanaticism, a glorious record was dimmed, the lustre of a precious heritage tarnished.

Stuyvesant was a bigot.   On February 1, 1656, he and his council issued an ordinance forbidding all meetings, whether public or private, differing from those of the Reformed Dutch Church.   Every person who took part in such meetings as preacher, reader or singer was fined one hundred pounds and every person found in such meetings twenty-five pounds.   This law, the first against liberty of conscience that disgraced the statute book of the colony was instigated by the two Dutch dominies, Johannes Megapolensis and Samuel Drisius. Stuyvesant saw to it that this statute remained no dead letter.   William Wickendam, a Baptist, was banished from the colony.   Robert Hodgson, a Quaker, was chained to a wheel barrow with a negro and, on his refusal to work, was beaten with a tarred rope until he fell to the ground.   But the law could not be enforced. Public opinion was against it.   The English at Flushing openly refused to obey it.   The West India Company disapproved of it and wrote Stuyvesant not to allow any more such statutes to be published, "but suffer the matter to pass in silence, and permit them free worship in their houses."   The observance of Sunday was strictly enjoined.   A number of ordinances were passed forbidding all unnecessary labor, sports, and the sale of liquor on that day.   That of 1661 relating to Wildwyck, provided that no person on Sunday should perform "any work at his ordinary business, whether plowing, sowing, mowing, threshing, winnowing, transporting wood, hay, straw, or grain, grinding or conveying any goods to or from the strand, on the penalty of one pound Flemish for the first time, double as much for the second time, and four times double as much for the third time." No one should give entertainment in taverns or "sell or give away, under any pretext whatsoever, beer, wine, or any strong drink," and if any one was found drunk on Sunday he was fined one pound Flemish for the benefit of the officer and should be confined in the watchhouse during the pleasure of the magistrates. The court enforced this ordinance. The Schout charged that Mathys Constapel (the gunner) tapped (sold drinks) on Sunday and he denied it. Pieter van Alen was fined for "receiving people and selling them brandy during the sermon." Aert Jacobsen was fined one pound Flemish for taking a load of beer to his house on Sunday. Aert Jansen was fined six guilders for having "fired a shot on Sunday during the sermon."

Proclamations appointing days of fasting, prayer and thanksgiving were usually issued once a year. On such days, "all exercises of playing tennis or ball, hunting, fishing, driving, ploughing, mowing, all illicit amusements as dicing and hard drinking during divine service" were prohibited. Capito, the Schout, demanded that the court punish Mattheu Blanshan because, "after the second beating of the drum, he churned some milk on the day of fasting and prayer. Defendant answers that the drum beat only once, and that he had no milk for his calf, and he never in his life did this before." His plea was of no avail. He was fined six guilders, one-half for the church. An ordinance provided that whereas, it was necessary that the youth from childhood up be instructed "in the principles and fundamentals of the Reformed religion," the children should after divine service, in the presence of the dominie and elders, be examined, "as to what they have committed to memory of the Christian commandments and Catechism, and what progress they have made; after which performance, the children shall be dismissed for that day, and allowed a decent recreation." With all the world calling to them to come out

of doors and play, think of those children, sitting there
on the butt end of a log, trying to answer questions such
as these:—

"What is thy only comfort in life and death?"
"Whence knowest thou thy misery?"
"What dost thou believe concerning the Holy Ghost?"
O poor little kids. O poor little kids.

They were pious people down there in Esopus. Away
back in 1658, in appealing to Stuyvesant for aid against
the Indians, they exclaim:—"Christ did not desert us,
but assisted and saved us and gave his own blood for
us, Christ has gathered us in one sheepfold, therefore
let us not desert each other, but rather help each other
to alleviate our sufferings." They met on Sundays at
the house of Jacob Jansen Stoll, where the scriptures
were read, psalms sung, and prayers offered. Andries
van der Sluys was precentor, i. e., leader, reader, chor-
ister. In 1660 Jacob Joosten, the court messenger, acted
in that capacity. There must have been trouble in
getting van der Sluys paid for his services for in 1664
Aert Martensen Doorn sues Cornelis Barentsen Slecht
for fifty guilders, "his share of the salary of the former
reader, Andries van der Sluys."

During Stuyvesant's visit to Esopus in 1658 he had
promised the people that their request for a dominie
would be complied with. He entered into correspon-
dence with the directors of the West India Company
with the result, that the Rev. Hermanus Blom, who had
been received into the Classis of Amsterdam January 4,
1655, was sent over, arriving at New Amsterdam in the
ship "de Otter" in 1659. Blom, with Dominie Megapolensis, who had been preaching at Fort Orange and New
Amsterdam, proceeded to Esopus, and on Sunday,
August 17, 1659, Blom preached in the morning and
afternoon. So well did the people like him that, on the
same day, Jacob Jansen Stoll, Thomas Chambers,
Juriaen Bestvaal, Jan Broersen, Dirck Goebsertsen,
Jacob Jansen Stoutenborgh, Jan Jansen, Hendrick

Cornelissen, Pieter Dircksen and Cornelis Barentsen Slecht addressed a letter to Stuyvesant requesting that Blom be appointed their pastor. They promised to "treat him decently" and in order that he should be able to sustain himself "and be more encouraged in his work" they agreed to make a good "bouwery" for him, "provide it with a house, barns, cows and other cattle as proper to tend the land" so that he might cultivate it himself or hire it out advantageously. If he left or if he should die the "bouwery" to remain for the support of a minister.

Blom returned to Amsterdam for his final examination and ordination. On February 16, 1660, he was examined by the Classis of Amsterdam and preached on the text, "But whoso keepeth his word, in him verily is the love of God perfected; hereby know we that we are in him. He that saith he abideth in him ought himself also so to walk, even as he walked. Brethren, I write no new commandment unto you, but an old commandment which ye had from the beginning. The old commandment is the word which ye have heard from the beginning."

The Classis liked the sermon and having passed the examination he was duly ordained "to the ministry with the laying on of hands" and sent to Esopus with the prayer, "the Almighty God, who has called this minister to the service of his church enrich him more and more with all talents and the blessings of his Holy Ghost, so that his labors may be crowned with abundant success, to the glory of his name, and salvation of men, and reward and adorn him, at the appearance of the great Shepherd of Sheep with the never fading crown of eternal glory."

Before leaving Amsterdam Blom married Anna Broeckhuysen. Blom returned to New Amsterdam in 1660. In consideration of the "cloth" Stuyvesant let him come in without payment of duties. Owing to the trouble with the Indians at Esopus he and Dominie Selyns, who had come over with him to be pastor at

Breuckelen, remained some time at New Amsterdam, for which Stuyvesant allowed them one beaver per week for board and lodging.

The directors of the company wrote Stuyvesant that Blom was sent over, "at a yearly salary of six hundred guilders, the balance up to one thousand or twelve hundred guilders, which is to be raised by the community must not be counted and paid to him by them, but by your honors, as chief magistrates, for reasons which your honors will easily comprehend; the proper manner in which this is to be carried out is left to your honors judgment."

Quite crafty. The company wanted Blom to understand that he was not only a servant of the Lord but their servant, as they did the paying. Blom arrived at Esopus September 5, 1660. He preached his first sermon September 12, 1660. On the 26th of December, of the same year, he administered the Lord's Supper to Anna Blom, Jacob Joosten, Jacob Burhans and Maddelyn Jorisse, his wife; Anton Crepel and Maria Blanschan, his wife; Andries Barentse and Hilletjen Hendricks, his wife; Margriet Chambrits, Roeloff Swartwout and Eva, his wife; Cornelis Slecht and Tryntje Tysse, his wife; Albert Roosa and Meylke de Jongh, his wife.

The first baptism recorded is that of Sophia, the child of Hendrick Martensen, of Coppenhage, soldier, and Margriet Meyringh or Meyers, his wife, on December 11, 1660. The first marriage, that of Jan Jansen, carpenter, and Catharyn Mattysen on October 3, 1660. Between 1660 and 1665 he baptised forty-eight children and married fourteen couples.

In 1661 the village built a parsonage for the dominie. It cost 3007.8 guilders ($1,202.96). Stuyvesant purchased six thousand bricks for it at Fort Orange. It was thatched with straw or reeds until 1669, when tile were used. Divine service was held in it until a church was erected. It was also used as a school house and for public purposes. Previous to its erection Blom had been

living in an upper room of the dwelling of Juriane Westvael, for which the village paid eighty florins rent. The
court imposed a fine of eighteen guilders on Thomas
Chambers for refusing to cart materials for the parsonage. As we have seen, in 1661, a land and excise
tax was levied to pay for the parsonage. It is evident
that the tax was not sufficient to cover the cost for in
1664 Fop Barense asked the court for fifty-seven and
one-half schepels of wheat and one hundred and fifty-
four guilders in wampum, amounts due for building the
parsonage, and Paulus Cornelisen wanted one hundred
and eight guilders in wampum for bricks for the same.
Jan Willemsen Hoochteyling, one of the deacons,
rendered an account showing that of the church money
one hundred and fifty-five guilders, thirty-five stivers in
wampum and from the poor money, three hundred and
fifty-nine guilders in wampum had been used for building the parsonage. He asked the court where he could
obtain payment and was politely informed by the magistrates that there was no money in the treasury, that they
had no authority to raise any and he must wait until
Stuyvesant came.

On March 4, 1661, Thomas Chambers, Cornelis Barentsen Slecht, Gertruy Andries, Roeloff Swartwout, Alaerdt
Heymensen Roose, and Juriaen Westvael agreed in
writing to give Blom as a salary for the first year, to
commence September 5, 1660, the "sum of 700 guilders
in corn, at beaver valuation, in case his farm should
fail, and we promise further to put the farm in good
order, according to contract, as soon as the land has
been allotted and to raise that sum at the latest for
the coming farming season. The subscribers to the
seven hundred florins were:

Thomas Chambers	fl 100	Dirck de Goier	fl. 20
Jacob Jansen Stoll	100	Hendrick Sewantryger.	20
Cornelis Slecht	50	Matys	20
Willem Jansen	50	Marten Harmensen	25

Jacob Jansen Stouten-		Jan de Backer........	12
bergh	50	Jan Broersen	15
Jan de Brabander......	15	Willem Jansen	30
Juriaen Westvael......	50	Albert Gouertsen	20
Pieter Dircksen........	60		

Blom's path at Wildwyck was not strewn with flowers. As we have seen, he got into a row with the magistrates as to whether they or the church should administer the estates of persons dying without heirs, in which controversy Stuyvesant decided against him. In those old days, as in the present, the dominie's salary was always in arrears. Then, as now, the people desired spiritual food but were backward in furnishing material provender to he who served it. In December, 1663, Deacon Roosa asked the court that the dominie be paid his salary because the consistory had made default. The magistrates held that as the contract of March 4, 1661, was only for a year the congregation should agree with Blom for the remaining years. The dominie was compelled to resort to the court and in this year obtained judgments against a number of his parishoners for their share of his salary, among whom was this same Deacon Roosa. In February, 1664, the dominie addressed a letter to the court, again asking for his pay, concluding as follows: "I leave it to the judgment of the Honorable Court here itself whether it is not a sad and grievous thing that a minister of the Word of God is, as here, compelled, with such trouble and pains, to seek for, and request of and through the court, his long since earned salary, the which has never been seen or heard of in Christendom." And in 1668, after his return to Holland, the good dominie, as he disappears from the records, plaintively appeals to the Rev. Classis "that a report may be made of his edifying ministry there (at Wildwyck) to the Hon. Directors of the West India Company, in the hope that something may be granted him on the arrears in his salary."

Dominie Blom was a brave man. An honest, conscientious man. None other would take his new-made wife out in the wilderness to preach the gospel of the Lord. He proclaimed the faith that was in him. A rare trait in these days. He fought with his people amid the smoke and flame of their homes in the Indian uprising of 1663 and, among the ruins, tenderly gave the consolation of his faith to the stricken. All honor to him and his memory. Here is a specimen of his eloquence:

"The Lord our God will make all turn out to the best for his church, and for the peace and quiet of the whole land. The mercy of our Lord Jesus Christ, the love of God the father, and the fellowship of the Holy Ghost be and remain with you, my worthy colleagues forever; and may the Triune God give us all together after this strife, the crown of immortal glory; and should we no more behold each other here, may we see each other hereafter in our Bridegroom's chamber, securely sheltered behind the blue curtains of the Heavens—in the third Heaven of Abraham's bosom, where shall be joy without sorrow, and a never ending gladness, always and forever; and receive altogether the hearty greeting of me who am one of the least of the servants of Christ Jesus in the work of the Lord."

CHAPTER XII

WILDWYCK AND ITS PEOPLE

THE Indians gave names to localities, mountains and streams descriptive of the same. In 1655, Stuyvesant called Esopus Waerinnewangh, evidently after the tribe Waerranawongs, who frequented the mouth of the Rondout Creek. The word probably means "hollowing," "concave site," "cove," "bay," descriptive of that locality.

Dominie Megapolensis, writing in 1657, says that eighteen miles up the North River there is a place called by the Dutch "Esopus or Sypous," by the Indians "Atharhacton." The word probably means, a large field, an extent of country, land cleared and ready for tillage, descriptive of the land about Esopus. The deed from the Indians to Thomas Chambers, August 5, 1657, calls the several parcels of land conveyed by it Machstapacick, Nachainekceck, Sepeeckcoe, Naranmapth, Wiwisowach-kick. Cornelis Barentsen Slecht, in his petition for a deed of land he had bought of the Indians, says it was called by them Wichquanis. In 1661, Volckert Jansen and Jan Thomasen purchased of the Indians half of "an island lying Eastwards in the Kill by aforesaid Volckert Jansen's and Jan Thomasen's bouwery, including the little island near by, called by the Indians Nano-seck, and by the Dutch, Little Cupper's Island.

The location of the stockade, as built in 1658, has been given in a previous chapter. The Rev. John Miller, who visited in Kingston in 1695, made a map of the village as it then existed. He says "it is quadrangular and stockaded round, having small horn works at convenient distances, one from the other, and in proper places. It is in circumference near as big as Albany, but as to number of houses not above half so big; on the south side there is a particular part, separated from the rest by a stockade, and strengthened by a block house and a horn works wherein are six guns." The "particular part" having an additional stockade was at about the corner of Wall and Main streets, now occupied by the church yard of the First Reformed Church, where stood the church and burying ground. The "small horn-works" were at North Front street and Clinton avenue; at about North Front and Green streets; at the corner of Main and Clinton avenue and on Green street at the head of John.

Dominie Blom, in his description of the Indian attack upon Wildwyck in 1663, says, "The houses were converted into heaps of stone." The dominie is speaking metaphorically. He was writing only five years after the building of the village in 1658. It is entirely clear from the records of the village that the dwellings of the people were log or board cabins of one story with a loft or garret. They had a chimney of stone or brick on the outside and a large open fireplace within. Some had wooden chimneys and others none, the fire being built on the floor, the smoke floating up through an opening in the roof. The houses were thatched with straw or reeds, which grew in inexhaustible quantities along the creek. At the time of the building of the stockade in 1658 the houses of the settlers, which were on both sides of the Esopus Creek, were torn down and moved within the stockade. This could hardly be if they were built of stone. The ordinances passed relating to dwellings clearly show how they were constructed. In 1659, the people of Wildwyck asked Stuyvesant that some order be made "regarding the thatch-roofs of houses, in which people live and make fires without chimneys." In 1661, an ordinance relating to Wildwyck was passed which provides that no person shall have any plastered or wooden chimneys, or kindle any fire in houses with walls or gables made of straw, or in the center on the floor of other houses covered with thatch, unless there be a good, solid plank ceiling and directs that fire wardens be appointed to inspect all chimneys. Brick and tile were used in building the parsonage, probably for the chimney and fireplace. This building, which was also used for the church and other public purposes, was thatched with straw or reeds. In July, 1669, the court ordered it be repaired and that it be covered with "straw or reed." In September of the same year this was reconsidered and it was ordered to be roofed with tiles. In 1662, Pieter de Rexmer sued Willem Jansen Stoll for "panes of glass sold and set" and in 1663 Huybrecht Bruyn brought an action against Jan Jansen for plastering walls, showing that conditions were improving. From all this it is clear that the old stone houses of which Kingston is so justly proud and which are all too fast disappearing are the product of a day later than that covered by this work.

The low lands bordering the Esopus Creek were devoid of forest and ready for the plow. For years they were the granary of the colony and the State. Even now their fertility is unsurpassed. As early as 1658 the farmers had sown nine hundred and ninety schepels (about 722 bushels) of wheat. A grist mill was necessary and one was built about 1661. It stood near the northwest corner of the stockade, the junction of the present Green and North Front streets. The power was furnished by what has since been known as the Tannery Brook, across which a dam was constructed. There was a gate in the stockade at this point and a road over the dam led to the New Village (Hurley). It was through this gate that the messenger rode on June 7, 1663, with the tidings that the New Village had been destroyed by the Indians. Pieter Jacobson was the miller. In 1661, his charges for grinding corn were fixed by the court at eight stivers (16 cents) per bushel, from those who had no wampum he could deduct the tenth part. On March 31, 1664, Pieter Jacobsen van Holsteyn and Pieter Cornelissen, partners, mortgaged "their mill" to Nicolaes Meyer, merchant at Manhattan, for sixty-one schepels of wheat. During the Indian war of 1663, the mill was used as a barrack for the troops. In the same year Jan Albertsen van Steenwyck was granted a lot "below the fort on the bank of the kill to the southward of Barent Gerritsen's, to be used as a tannery and garden."

At the time of building the stockade in 1658, three carpenters came from Fort Orange, whom Stuyvesant had hired "to make a bridge over the kill." In September of the same year it was, with the exception of one beam, swept away by a freshet so that it could not be repaired, and the farmers were not willing to build a new one before winter. Some local historians state that this bridge was over the Esopus Creek. They are mistaken. The bridge was over the Tannery Brook near the northwest corner of the stockade. This brook was,

COMMERCIAL BEGINNING OF NEW YORK.

within the memory of some now living, a considerable stream. As has been stated, it furnished sufficient power for a mill. The Esopus Creek was at least a quarter of a mile from the village. The settlers on its further side had removed their dwellings within the stockade. There would be no necessity for a bridge except to reach the lands on the other side of the creek, which was done for many years thereafter, by fording. Besides the Esopus was a large stream, given to sudden and very high freshets, to bridge it in those early days was too much of an undertaking for a few settlers with limited appliances. Just when another bridge was built over "the kill" the records do not state.

In March, 1662, Cornelis Barentsen Slecht sued Geertruyt Andrisse for one hundred forty-six guilders, ten stivers, "heavy money" advanced for building "the bridge." In 1663 Schout Swartwout complained that Aert Jacobsen had spoken disrespectfully of the court "at the bridge." In the same year the Schout asked the court to fine Henderick Jochemsen for having violated the ordinance of June 4, 1663, "in that he was in the field near the bridge without permission and a convoy." The defendant admitted "that he was at the bridge, as a sentry, as he with others present had to repair the bridge, but being unable to work because of a lame hand he therefore stood sentry for the laborers."

The records furnish no testimony that there were any residents within the present limits of Ulster County, except in and about Wildwyck and the New Village, up to the time of the surrender to the English in 1664, except possibly "the old sawyer." The records do not disclose his name but the story has long been told that "the old sawyer" in the early days lived upon the bank of the Hudson near the mouth of the Esopus creek in the present town of Saugerties. Captain Cregier's journal of the Indian war of 1663 mentions some Catskill Indians being near "Sagers Kill." This stream, called the Saw kill or Sawyers kill, is in the northern part of the town of Saugerties and empties into the Hudson near the mouth of the Esopus creek at Saugerties village. The act of 1683 dividing the province of New York into counties makes this stream the northern boundary of Ulster County and the southern boundary of Albany County. On June 26, 1663, de Desker writes Stuyvesant that the Catskill Indians had said that the Dutch at Wildwyck should keep quiet "else all the houses on this side the Sagerskil would be burned." In the same year Cregier informs Stuyvesant that all the Indians above "Sagertjen" had agreed not to harm the Dutch. In the treaty of 1677 between Governor Andros and the Indians, by which they cede lands north of Kingston, it is stated that the Chief Kaeleop declared, "that he had ceded to the 'old sawyer' his claim upon a kill, called the 'Sawyer's Kill,' and the land stretching up to the boundary of the land belonging to the Katskil Indians along the river as far as the mountains above." In a survey of what is now the greater part of the village of Saugerties, made by order of Governor Deagan in 1785, the land is described as "being a piece of land called the Sagiers." A very careful writer upon all that pertains to the early history of Ulster County says that he has identified the "old sawyer" with Barent Cornelis Volge—also spelled "Vogel." That he has come into possession of an ancient deed, dated April 10, 1684, given by Volge to Richard Heyes, in which Volge describes himself as "late upon Hudson's river near Esopus, Sawyer." The deed conveys to Heyes—"a certain tract or parcell of land commonly knowne by the name of the Sargertuys Scituate, lyeing and being at a certaine Creeke or kill commonly called the Mother Kill and thence Runing along the said Hudson's river northerly to a Certaine small Island called by the name of Wanton Island, and from thence Due west into woods into the hills or Mountaines and sem along the same mountaines Southerly to the said Mother Kill and see down the said kill to the mouth thereof, where the land first began." The deed states that the land had been conveyed to Volge by Christopher Davis and Andrews Devors, date not given. It also recites that Volge had:—"Made great improvement thereon by building of houses, barns, Stables and Saw mills, all of which were unhappily Destroyed by the Indians. Since which, that is to say, in the years of our Lord, 1683, the Aforesaid Cornelisse built Another House upon the same for further Improvement of the Premisses."

The mystery that surrounds the "old sawyer" is not whether such a person existed but whether he carried on the business of a sawyer, had a saw mill on the Saw creek as early as the time he is first mentioned. According to the above deed the establishment of Volge was an extensive one. If it existed the settlers at Wildwyck must have known of it. If there was a mill why did Stuyvesant, in 1658, go to the trouble to go away up to Fort Orange for plank for the guard house? When was the plant destroyed? During the Indian troubles of 1655 or during the wars of 1659 or 1663? In all the voluminous record of the period there is not a word concerning such a plant or even that there was a settler in Ulster County north of Wildwyck. The deed to Volge does not state when the buildings had been erected or when destroyed. It was given twenty years after the "old sawyer" first appears in the record. However the question may be answered one fact remains. His memory is secure. His cognomen still lives in the name of the village and the town of Saugerties.

Wherever a Dutchman went the bell of a school house soon rang. At a time when half the population of England could neither read or write Holland had her universities and her colleges and above all placed the spelling book and the reader in the hands of every child. In 1658 Andries van der Sluys taught the children of Esopus reading and writing. In 1660 and 1662 Jacob Joosten was schoolmaster. In 1666 Willem La Montagnie conducted a day and night school both winter and summer.

The population of Wildwyck and the New Village can only be approximately stated. At the time of building the stockade in 1658 there were "thirty fighting men" and a total of sixty or seventy people. In February, 1660, Stuyvesant stated to his council that the Esopus contained two or three villages, "each of twenty to twenty-four families." After the massacre of June 7, 1663, there were "sixty-nine efficient men."

Lots at Wildwyck were granted to forty-five different persons. Up to the time of the surrender to the English in 1664 land patents had been issued to sixteen persons other than those to whom lots had been granted. The excise tax of 1661 was levied against sixty-seven persons and the land tax of the same year against thirty-four. From all the data the total population at the time of the surrender to the English in 1664 was between two hundred and two hundred and fifty. The population was a cosmopolitan one. There were Dutch, English, French and German. The representatives of the last three wielded the greater influence in affairs.

Up to the time of the surrender to the English in 1664 the following patents or grants of land had been made to the below mentioned persons. A morgen is a little over two acres.

1653, Nov. 8, Thomas Chambers, Esopus, 38 morgens.

1654, Aug. 29, Juriaen Westphael, Esopus, 32½ morgens.

1656, Sept. 25, Christoffel Davits, Esopus, 36 morgens.

1657, March 27, Johan de Laet, widow of Johan de Hulter, Esopus, 500 morgens.

1662, March 10, Thomas Chambers, "Pissemans Hoek," Esopus, 4½ morgens.

1662, Dec. 7, Cornelis Barentsen Slecht, Esopus, 25 morgens.

1663, April 16, G. G. van Schaick and others, a new town, Esopus, 33 morgens.

1663, April 20, Philip Pieterse Schuyler, a new town, Esopus, 34 morgens.

1663, April 25, Jan Broersen and others, Wildwyck, 25 morgens.

1663, April 25, Jan de Wever, Esopus, 21 morgens.

1663, April 25, Anthony Crepel (Crispell), Kaelacp's land, Esopus, 8 morgens.

1663, J. Jans Oesterout, a lot, Wildwyck.

1663, Matys Blanchan, a lot, Wildwyck.

1663, April 25, Cornelis Wynkoop, near Esopus, 12 morgens.

1663, April 25, Louis DuBois, near Esopus, 20 morgens.

1663, April 25, Roeloff Swartwout, near Esopus, 20 morgens.

1663, April 25, Henderick Cornelise, van Holsteyn, near Esopus, 2 morgens.

1663, April 25, Lambert Huyberts (Brink), near Esopus, 21 morgens.

1663, April 26, Jan Tomassen, near Esopus, 33 morgens.

1663, April 28, Volckert Jans, 33 morgens.

1663, Dec. 10, Nicolaes Varleth, Esopus, 21 morgens.

1664, April 22, Thomas Chambers, Esopus, 22 morgens.

1664, May 12, Margaret, wife of Chambers, 48 morgens.

1664, May 17. Fredrick Philips, lot, Wildwyck.

1664, Aug. 19, Petrus Bayard, Esopus, 130 morgens.

1664, Aug. 19, Albert Heymans Roose (Roosa), a plantation, Esopus.

The patent to Johan de Laet was claimed to cover the village of Wildwyck, but this was denied by Stuyvesant.

The patents to van Schaick, Schuyler, Crepel, Wynkoop, DuBois, Swartwout, van Holsteyn, Brink, Tomassen, and Volokert Jans were for land at the New Village (Hurley).

The cows were pastured in one common herd under the charge of a "cowherder." Catelyn, the Walloon, complained to the court that the cowherder did not drive her cows home in time and that he did not drive them home for two days. He replied that as she did not drive her cows to the herd, he could not take care of them. The court rendered the very sensible judgment that, "Catelyn shall drive her cows to the herd and that the defendant shall then take care of them."

Many of these pioneers could not write. They signed by making their mark. In this connection it should be remembered that each person chose a particular mark and always used it in signing instruments. His mark was synonymous with his name and is the most certain way of identifying persons bearing the same name.

Some of the people indulged in the luxury of linen shirts, the boys wore "leather breeches," while the women decked themselves with ribbons.

In 1657 the directors of the West India Company wrote Stuyvesant that "a redoubt at the Esopus" would be advantageous but the finances of the company would not permit it. Stuyvesant, however, went ahead and in 1660 a redoubt or fort was built on the Rondout creek, near its mouth.

Some soldiers were kept there and an officer to see that no liquors went to the village until they were entered with Jacob Burhans, the collector of the excise. After its erection the Dutch called the place "Rondhout.' Authorities differ as to the meaning of the word Rondout. One that it means "standing timber." Another that it is a commercial term for "masts" or round timber, but is never applied to standing timber. That the Dutch used the term palisades for logs set in the ground to form a stockade and also used the word "blockhuys" for a blockhouse so that there is no reason for thinking that the fort was called Rondout because it was built of logs or protected by palisades. That there is no Dutch word corresponding to redoubt. That the Dutch used the French term "redoute," pronounced in the French way. Another that the word has sometimes been derived from the Dutch "rondeel," meaning a round tower at the corner of a fortification. Another eminent Dutch scholar that the word would seem to be derived from the Dutch "rounduit," meaning "roundly out" or "out round," but what connection that could have with a fort on the creek it is difficult to see. Whatever may be the meaning of the word it has been perpetuated in the name of the former village of Rondout and the Rondout creek. Nearly every one drank brandy and beer. The excise tax which was collected from all who purchased liquors was levied against sixty-seven persons, nearly all the adult male population. Dominie Blom paid fifty florins, only exceeded by Hendrick Jochems, seventy-five florins; Jacob Burhans, seventy-one florins; Barent Gerritzen, sixty-five florins; Cornelis Barentsen Slecht, seventy florins; and Thomas Chambers, eighty-four florins.

Barent Gerritsen and Mattheu Blanchan ran brandy distilleries, and Slecht a brewery. Mathys Roelefsen sued Aert Aertson Otterspoor; Jonas Ransou sued Evert Pals; Storm Albertsen sued Baerent Gerritsen; Elassjan Ransou sued Pieter Hillebrantss for brandy sold to them. Jonas Ransou owned up that he owed Elsjen Jans for "one can of brandy, one turkey, and three musjens (half pints) of brandy." Pieter van Alen was fined for selling brandy "during the sermon." Jan Baronse Amersfort and Sara Gilliasen were fined for smuggling liquors.

The Schout charged Mattheu Blanchan, who had a distillery, with violating the ordinance forbidding distillers from selling at retail in that he had sold, "a half anker of brandy to his brother-in-law, Lowys Dubo" (DuBois). The entire court went on horseback to the New Village and found the brandy at the house of DuBois. Blanchan was fined one hundred and twenty-five guilders, "one third to the poor, one third to the bench and one-third to the Schout. Blanchan appealed to the Court at New Amsterdam. Its magistrates wrote the court at Wildwyck that Stuyvesant had said that Blanchan owed no fine. They therefore advised that the matter between the Schout and Blanchan "be arranged and settled in love and friendship."

Here is an inventory, taken in 1663, of the property left by Hendrick Leoman. One gelden, one large brewing kettle, one sword and belt, one trunk without key, wherein was found, one letter case containing letters, and a note book with memoranda of outstanding debts and accounts, one old gray suit, one old gray colored pair of breeches, one new gray suit, two pair black woolen stockings, one new black hat and hat box, one bar lead, four small pieces of Haarlem cloth, one clothes brush, one trunk, two cravats, three handkerchiefs, one package containing about a pound of lead, one wagon frame, with iron tires."

Stuyvesant's proclamation of March 24, 1660, appointing that day as a day of fasting and prayer throughout the colony forbade all "illicit amusements as dicing and hard drinking" during divine service on that day shows some of the "amusements" of the people. On February 12, 1664, Dominie Blom, in the name of the consistory of the church, petitioned the magistrates of Wildwyck: "that the public, sinful and scandalous Bacchanalian days of Bastenseen (Shrove Tuesday), coming down from the heathens from their idol Bacchus, the god of wine and drunkenness, being also a leaven of Popery, inherited from the pagans, which the Apostle, in I Cor. 5, admonishes true Christians to expurge, may, while near at hand, be prescribed in this place by your Honors." The court informed the dominie that it would be glad to comply with the request "so far as its instructions permit." This petition probably was aimed against the custom long prevalent "among the farmers of Gelderland and the borders of the Rhine to assemble at Shrovetide to 'Pull the Goose,' which custom was introduced into New Netherland as early as 1654. On such occasions a goose, whose neck and head had been previously smeared with oil or soap, was fastened by a rope between two poles. Horsemen then entered the lists and, driving at full gallop, made an attempt to seize the prize. They would often miss their mark and fall to the ground. He who succeeded in bearing off the goose was declared king of the festival." Then, as now, the servant girl was a problem hard to solve. Gritodgen Hillebrants asked the court why her master, Juriaen Westgaer, discharged her. He replied that "when he was sick she went out every day and returned home late at night, and that he then said to her, 'where you have been during the day, go there also at night.'" The court would not listen to any such plea and ordered him to pay her "a quarters year's wages."

The people of Wildwyck were rather sensitive as to their reputation. Barent Gerritsen pommeled Hey Olfersen because he called him a scoundrel. Hey Olfersen charged Hester Douwens with calling him a thief. She told the court: "This is plain enough, because he took out of my house at night some flour and some pieces of meat, as set forth in the summons. I also miss a beaver, an otter, and a half beaver, as well as an anker of small beer, and the person who stole the one I guess must also have taken the other." Hey said he had taken some meat and flour at night because he was hungry "as she would not give me food and I was working for her I tried to procure it, since there was little or no food for sale here." The court let Hey out on bail that he might prepare his case and suspended judgment until the arrival of the "Noble Lord General." Hester pursued Hey even in his grave, for in September, 1663, she appeared in court, demanding seven schepels of wheat that his estate owed her.

On July 4, 1662, Mathys Blanchan appeared before the court and demanded vindication of his honor. He said: "That Juriaen told his wife that it was reported that Dirck Adriaensen said to her he had seen Matheu Blanchan beat Juriaen Westvael's pig. Defendant Juriane Westvael and his wife admit having heard this from Dirck Adriaensen, and state that Pieter Janson also heard it. Defendant Dirck Adriaensen denies this, and says he did not say so. The Schout and Commissaries order the parties to preserve the peace, and sentence

Dirck Adriaensen to pay a fine of six guilders for the poor."

Gysbert van Imbrogh sued Altsen Sybrants for calling him a Jew and a sucker. She defended upon the ground that he had called her a heap of dung.

Tryntje, the wife of Slecht, told the court that she was sorry that she had called the "Noble Lord Johan de Decker a bloodsucker." "She spoke while depressed and discouraged because of the many misfortunes that had befallen her through the savages." The court preferred "mercy to the severity of justice" and therefore fined her only twenty-five guilders in wampum, "for the benefit of the church."

Paulus Paulusen sued Eva Swartwout for saying he stole twelve chickens. Gerret Fooken and Pieter Cornelissen testified that they "did not personally hear that plaintiff stole twelve chickens from her, but that they heard that she said, while plaintiff chased a hen out of the barn, 'Whoever would do the one would do the other.' "

The wife of Cornelis Barentsen Slecht was midwife of the village.

The court records are almost entirely free of complaints for criminal offenses. None of the graver crimes, murder, arson, rape, or burglary appear. Those that were made were almost all for assault and it is evident that the parties charged were simply "on a spree." This is a most remarkable fact and speaks volumes for the character of the people.

Thomas Chambers was charged with wounding Jan Jansen, his brother-in-law, with a knife.

Jonas Ransou charged Mathys Roeloofsen with "murderously attacking him at night." Hey Olfersen complained that Barent Gerretsen "beat and kicked him and trampled upon him." The defendant admitted it and said that he did it because Hey called him a scoundrel. The court referred the matter to arbitrators. The Schout charged Paulus Tomassen with assaulting him and threatening to shoot him. The defendant said he was drunk and does not know what occurred. The court ordered defendants to settle with the Schout "or to work one month on the dam, at his own expense, and to pay all costs that have been incurred; and in case he cannot arrive at a settlement with the Schout, that he shall give bail to the court against running away, or shall be chained while working on the dam." On November 20, 1663, the Schout complained that Tjerck Glaesen (de Witt), who was then a magistrate, was armed with a knife in the house of Albert Gysbertsen and acted "as if he wished to kill every man, woman, and child." The court advised that as defendant had settled with Gysbertsen "he shall remain away from the bench until he shall have settled and adjusted this matter with the Schout." The parties must have got together because on December 18, DeWitt is once more upon the bench.

The following are the values and quantities of the Dutch coin, weights and measures referred to in this work: A stiver; two cents. A guilder, forty cents. A pound Flemish, two dollars and forty cents. A daelder, sixty cents. A Dutch mile, 4.611 statute miles. A morgen, 2.103 acres. An anker, 10 gallons. A schepel, 0.764 bushels, about three pecks. A muddle, four schepels. A musjen, a half pint. A vim, a stack of 104 to 108 sheaves of grain.

As we have seen in the chapter devoted to "Government," little if any coin circulated in the colony. A beaver was the standard of value, and was worth about eight guilders, $3.40. Wampum was the circulating medium. Its value was fixed by ordinance and constantly fluctuated between six or eight white and three or four black beads for a stiver. All financial transactions were carried on in wampum, wheat or other grain. Wheat in 1663 was worth about thirty cents a bushel; at Wildwyck, in 1664, ninety cents. Three schepels of oats were worth one of wheat. The following are some of the prices paid at Wildwyck: Two cows, two hundred guilders in corn. One cow, one hundred and fifteen guilders. A pig, five and six schepels of wheat. A team of horses, four hundred guilders in wheat. Another team, six hundred guilders, beaver value. One horse, one hundred and six schepels of wheat. An anker of brandy, forty schepels in oats. An anker of wine, eighty guilders in wampum. A hat, six schepels of wheat. A pair of shoes, one half schepel of wheat. Three blankets, eleven guilders each. Two and one quarter ells duffels, seven guilders, four stivers. Two thousand brick, two muddle of wheat. Rent of a farm for five years, two thousand guilders. Rent of a house, four guilders per month. Rent of a house for a year, forty guilders. A house, barn and lot sold for seven hundred guilders in wheat and oats. Land sold for ten or twelve guilders per morgen. Interest ranged from ten to twelve per cent. Two days mowing grass, two schepels of wheat. One day's work, two guilders in wampum. Putting up two brandy stills, an axle with which to grind, and a malt kiln, fourteen schepels of wheat. Threshing per day, one guilder, ten stivers in wampum. Harvesting, two guilders, ten stivers in wampum. Making a plow, three beavers. Wages of a boy for the first year, ten schepels of wheat and a pair of "leather breeches." For the second year, fifteen schepels of wheat. Thirteen days' carpenter work, ten schepels of wheat. The Sergeant of the militia got twenty guilders per month, the soldiers eight to ten guilders. The fare from Manhattan to Wildwyck for a man, his wife and children was sixteen guilders in wampum.

Gysbert van Imborch sued Gerret Fooken for "a quantity of thirty-three and one-half schepels of wheat due him from defendant and his partner, Jan Gerretsen, in which sums are included six schepels of wheat for shaving and doctor's bill for Jan Gerrets, for a whole year. He also demands from defendant two schepels of wheat for doctor's fee during his sickness after said time."

Here is Doctor Imboroch's library: In folio, a Dutch Bible. History of Emanuel Van Meteren. Titus Livinus, in Dutch. Medicine book of Christopher Wirtsungh. Medicine book of Johannes DeVigo. Medicine book of Ambrosius Paree. Book on the mixing of wine. A Versaly & Valuerda Anatomy. Frederick Henry of Nassau, his life and works. In Quarto, Johan Sarcharson. General exhibit of Holy Writ. Bacchus Wonderworks. Bernhard Van Sutphen Practice. Sebastian Frank's World's Mirror. Receuil of Amsterdam. A German (work on) medicine and products of art. A written medicine book. A German manual of the Catholic Faith. Another written medicine book. Redress of the nobility of Holland by Johan Geul. In Octavo, Two books on the perfection and perspicuity of the Word of God, by Albert Hutteman. A French Catechism. Bee-hive of Aldegonde. Arithmetic, by Jan Belot Dieppois. Chronicles of the lives and works of the Kings of England. Medical remarks by Nicolaes Tulp. German medical manual, by Q. Apollinaron. d'Argenis, by J. Barckilaj. Confession of faith, by P. Paulus Van Venetien. Treatise on the faith, by Henry Hexman. Examination of surgery, by Mr. Cornelis Herls. A written medicine and student book. German song book. Book on surgery, without a title. Arithmetic, by Sybrand Hansen Cardinael. In Duodecimo, Characteristics of the children of God. Jan Taffin. The Golden Harp. Royal road to Heaven. Two tracts, by Petrus Molinej. Meditations on the 51st Psalm. Twelve "Devotions," by Philip Kegel, in German.

School books in quarto, 8 Stories of David. 3 last wills. 17 beautiful proofs of man's misery. 3 General Epistles.

School books in octavo, 100 Catechisms. 23 Stories of Joseph. 102 A. B. C. Books. 27 Arts of Letters. 19 large "Succinct Ideas." 20 small "Succinct Ideas."

9 "steps" of youth. 13 proofs of human misery. 8 books of the Gospel and the Epistles. 48 "Succinct Ideas," by Jacobus Borstius. 1 "Short Way," by Megapolensis.

Among other effects left by the doctor were, a barber's saw, a wig with a wreath, a wine glass with pewter foot, a barber's grindstone and a blue shaving towel.

At the auction of his property in 1665 a schepel of wheat was valued at six guilders, of rye at four and one-half guilders, buckwheat, three guilders; oats, two guilders; barley, four guilders; white peas, four guilders; gray peas, five guilders; a milch cow sold for one hundred and fifty guilders; two milch goats and a young buck sixty-four guilders; three winter hogs, two males and one female, twenty-one guilders.

CHAPTER XIII

AFTERMATH

THE city of Kingston is usually called that Old Dutch Town. Its early settlers are devoutly believed to have been simon-pure Dutchmen and their descendants are very proud of their lineage. In part, this is true. But it is a misnomer. The Amsterdam of the old world and the Amsterdam of the new were as cosmopolitan as New York City is to-day. They were the abode of nearly every race and cities of refuge for every persecuted sect, Catholic, Protestant, Quaker and Jew. This was true, to the extent of its population, of Esopus and Wildwyck. While the Dutch element predominated, other nationalities were represented and these constituted many of the most prominent and influential citizens. Matthew Blanschan, Louis DuBois, Anthony Crispell, Nicolas DePuy, the Hasbrouck brothers and others were French. Every Pels, a Pomeranian. Hendrick Schoonmaker, a German; Pieter and Huybrecht Bruyn, Norwegians. Christopher Davis, William Carpenter and others, English. Above and beyond all the first pioneer, he who led these Argonauts to the new El Dorado, the most influential man in the settlement, he whose word went further than even that of Stuyvesant, was the red-headed English carpenter, Thomas Chambers.

While it does not fall within the period covered by this history, it may be well to briefly relate the story of the planting of the village of New Paltz, about sixteen miles south of Kingston, as it concerns many of the first settlers of Wildwyck. In the Indian war of 1663, when Wildwyck and the New Village (Hurley) were burned, among those carried away captives by the Indians were the wife and three children of Louis Du-Bois, two children of Matthew Blanschan and the wife and child of Anthony Crispell. The story of the expedition led by Captain Kregier to rescue the captives has been told in Chapter VII. Among his company was Louis DuBois and Anthony Crispell. This small armed force followed the Wallkill river to the present town of Shawangunk where they found the fort of the Indians, which was destroyed. The captives were rescued and the power of the Indians forever broken so they ceased to be a terror and a menace to the whites.

Between this time and 1677, Jean and Abraham Hasbrouck, Louis Bevier, Hogo Freer, Christian Deyo and others had settled at Kingston or Hurley. All of these, including Louis DuBois and many of the early settlers were French Huguenots from the Palatinate, that ill-defined territory roughly embraced in what in 1871 was Alsace and Lorraine and Wurtenburg in Germany. They desired a home by themselves in which they could freely speak their own language, practice their own religion and have their peculiar manners and customs. Louis DuBois and those who had been in the expedition of 1663 had not forgotten the beautiful valley of the Wallkill. So in 1677 Louis DuBois, Abraham DuBois, Isaac Du-Bois, Christian Deyo, Pierre Deyo, Abraham and Jean Hasbrouck, Andrew and Simon LeFevre, Louis Bevier, Anthony Crispell and Hugo Freer purchased of the Indians a tract of land lying in the present town of New

Paltz on both sides of the Wallkill river. This purchase was afterwards confirmed by patent of Governor Andros. Thus was laid the foundation of the village of New Paltz, named from the "Pfals," as they called the Palatinate. Other Huguenots found here a home and for many years it continued to be a French Huguenot settlement. Its settlers and many, very many of their descendants were strong, able men, who in large measure, have shaped and controlled the history of Ulster County.

A word to those who are interested in tracing their descent from the Dutch. Because the name you bear appears in the Dutch records and sounds Dutch, do not be sure that it is so. The Dutchmen who kept the records spelled an English, French or German name phonetically, thus making it appear to be a Dutch name. In using the records the system of nomenclature employed by the Dutch should be kept in mind. They had, except in few instances, no surnames. Those who had seldom used them. A person's name was simply John, or Peter or Hendrick. John had a son who was named Cornelis and it would be written Cornelis Johnsen. That is, "sen" or "se" would be added to the name of the father, signifying the son of. Cornelis would have a son named Martin. His name would not be written Marten Johnsen but Martin Cornelisen or Cornelise. You would search the records in vain for a Martin Johnson. The Dutch "van" means "of" or "from" and was used to designate the place from whence the person came or the place of his residence or nativity. Thus the name of the first Van Buren who came to this country was Cornelis Maesen, that is Cornelis the son of Maes, the Dutch for Thomas. He sailed from Holland in 1631 and settled at Rensselaerswyck, now Albany. His name appears in the log-book of the ship in which he sailed from Holland as Cornelis Maessen van Buren, thus designating that he came from the Province of Buren in Holland. The names of neither of his children are written Van Buren. Thus the son Martin is Martin Cornelissen, never Martin

Maessen, or Martin Van Buren. It is not until the grandchildren of Cornelis Maessen that Van Buren was adopted and used as the family name.

This is true of all the "Vans." It does not follow that the particular "Van" whose name you bear was a Dutchman. Holland, as has been said, was very cosmopolitan, and the Van Buren, or Van Etten, or Van Slyke or any other of the many "Vans" may simply mean the place from which he sailed or in which he lived. The high-sounding "Van" from whom you trace your descent of which you are so proud may have been some very common John of almost any nationality. My paternal ancestor Cornelis Maessen, came to this country under a contract with Kiliaen Van Rensselaer, to work for him for three years, "no exception as to any kind of work being made" at his manor of Rensselaerswyck. His coat of arms must have been an axe, a shovel, a pick, a hoe and a flint lock.

But few of the Dutch settlers could write. They signed documents by making their mark. Each person had his own particular mark. The most certain way of identifying one person from another who has the same name is by a comparison of such marks.

The Dutch were a strong people. They had spent centuries in wresting their half-submerged land from the waters of the ocean. Over a century in a struggle with the most powerful nation in Europe to achieve liberty for themselves and their children. They were educated far beyond any other people of Europe. They were brave, honest, frugal, pertinacious, intensely conservative, strictly kept the conjugal tie, believed in an ever-living God and their religious creed. They were afraid of and bent the knee to no man. Such were the people who settled the land of the Esopus and peopled the valley of the Hudson. They have left their impress upon every page of the history of the Empire State and, in large measure, their influence has controlled, shaped and fashioned the path that the Great Republic has trod.

In order to know the real history of Wildwyck we must know who and what its people were. What did they do. How did they live. What were their beliefs and their ideals. What were they striving to accomplish. These matters I have endeavored to portray in the preceding pages. Let us briefly recapitulate. Why did they come to the Esopus. I have told you that the first settlers came from Rensselaerswyck. Go read the lease between Kiliaen van Rensselaer, its patroon, and Thomas Chambers and you will receive your answer. His tenants were his serfs, his slaves, his chattels. The blood of an Englishman ran in the veins of Chambers. For generations his fathers had asserted that across the threshold of their homes even the King of England could not pass without permission. And those Dutchmen up there. They were the descendents of the men and women who for over a hundred years had battled for freedom, for the right to govern themselves without the aid of prince, king or emperor. And so, to attain liberty, freedom, for the right to plant their feet upon a spot of ground and to say to all the world hands off, this is mine, they braved every danger, faced every peril and came down to the land of the Esopus.

They lived in small log huts thatched with straw or reeds. They wore coarse clothes and in winter were clothed in skins. They subsisted upon a little grain, pork, beef, game and fish. They were afraid of neither man, God or the devil, but they laid deep the foundation of the Empire State.

At a time when over one-half the population of England could neither read or write, Holland had her colleges and her universities and above and beyond all, her public schools. The blood of the fatherland asserted itself. One of the first things these Dutchmen did was to employ a teacher for their children. They knew that the school house was the cradle of liberty. They wished their children to have a better education than they had enjoyed. They desired that every child should have an equal chance with every other child. The bell of every school house that rings out in the Great Republic is rung by the spectral hand of a Dutchman.

These pioneers were Godfearing men and women. To them the Bible was really the word of God. Higher criticism had not yet appeared. To them the Dominie was really the servant of God. He was reverenced and obeyed. His opinions were respected and upon nearly every question turned the scale. He was the leading man of the community and guided and in part controlled all that was done. The church and this old faith moulded and fashioned their lives. It lifted them to a nobler level and a higher plane. It made them better, purer men and women. It sustained them in every hour of trial and every hour of peril and to its influence we can trace nearly all the good they accomplished.

Some of these pioneers brought their wives with them. Others married here. The record contains but little concerning the woman of Wildwyck. From scattered data in the records and musty old papers her portrait may be truly painted. She had large hands, large feet and was usually of very ample proportions. She never dreamed of trying to reduce fat. Go down to New York and watch the immigrants land and you will see thousands very much like her. She was what the dainty dame of to-day would describe as rough, coarse, ignorant, uncultivated. If she were here to-day there are but few, very few women who boast of belonging to polite society and of their descent from this same woman who would dream of inviting her to their table, yet, in large measure, she made possible the sumptuous home they enjoy. But she was a woman in all that the word implies. She assisted her husband build their log hut, plant the grain and gather the crops. She was a good cook and there was rarely a servant in her home. In the absence of the men, at the appearance of the Indian, she grasped the rifle, gathered her children about her and defended them even unto death. She reared her children to reverence God, to go to church, to become decent, pure, honest men and women. She had no other thought than the welfare of her family and her home. In short, she was what God Almighty designed a woman to be—the noblest, the holiest thing on earth, the helpmate of her husband and the mother of mankind. Such is the picture of these old settlers as I read it in the records. May their virtues be emulated by us. Their sins have long ago been forgiven and forgotten.